With love

Mother

1973

DEAR BERTRAND RUSSELL ...

BY BERTRAND RUSSELL

by Harold White F.I.I.P., F.R.P.S.

DEAR
BERTRAND RUSSELL...

A selection of his correspondence
with the general public 1950 – 1968

INTRODUCED AND EDITED BY
BARRY FEINBERG
AND
RONALD KASRILS

London
GEORGE ALLEN AND UNWIN LTD
RUSKIN HOUSE MUSEUM STREET

FIRST PUBLISHED IN 1969
SECOND IMPRESSION 1970

© *George Allen & Unwin Ltd* 1969

ISBN 0 04 826003 7

PRINTED IN GREAT BRITAIN
in 11 *on* 12 *pt Plantin*
BY WESTERN PRINTING SERVICES LTD
BRISTOL

ACKNOWLEDGEMENTS

We are indebted to Bertrand Russell and the Bertrand Russell Peace Foundation for permission to publish his letters, and to the good offices of Continuum Ltd of London who sponsored this work and, together with McMaster University, Ontario, allowed us free and unlimited access to the Russell Archives from which the material of this book was gathered. We also take this opportunity to thank the many individuals from a host of countries extracts of whose letters appear in this book. Finally, we are grateful to Ken Blackwell for his expert bibliographical advice.

PREFACE BY BERTRAND RUSSELL

The letters in this volume were written without any thought that they would ever be published. They recall some of the lighter moments of distraction from answering more serious correspondence, although I thought them sufficiently important to write and welcome their publication.

Undoubtedly the art of letter-writing has been lost in the twentieth century through the development of the telephone and, to a lesser extent, the greater ease of travel. In my youth it was imperative to master the art of letter-writing if one was to make one's way in the world. Letters had a formality which today must appear ponderous and even absurd. When my grandfather wrote to my father he would conclude 'Yrs. aff., Russell'. Every letter had a formal beginning and a formal ending, and even to a close friend one might end as follows: 'I sincerely trust that you and your family are in the best of health and that you are not displeased by the course of events in the great world. For my part I am enjoying the sunshine and have every hope of profiting by it. With warmest good wishes, I remain, Yours very truly . . .'.

The owner of a coal-mine seeking financial assistance from the Prime Minister or other leading Minister might have written:

'My Lord, I am venturing to approach Your Lordship on a somewhat delicate matter. The matter in question is the working of the coal-mine at Z. Your Lordship will doubtless have realised not only through the public press but also through private communications that the coal in this area is giving out unless forcibly encouraged by public money. Your Lordship is also doubtless aware that great hardship will be caused to all classes of the community in the neighbourhood of Z unless steps are taken and taken soon to mitigate the impending disaster. Trusting that Your Lordship enjoys good health, and continues to enjoy the confidence of the Party, I remain Your Lordship's humble and devoted servant . . .'.

One was never so brash as to ask for money bluntly, but the purpose of the letter was not lost on its recipient. It was a world remote from the age of the tape recorder, the telex machine and

9

the 'hot line', and I cannot say that its passing necessarily denotes progress. Today favours are still sought in clubs and over lunch, but the growth of bureaucracies has produced a new form of letter which is archaic, deliberately uninformative and completely lacking in subtlety. The Civil Service rule books on letter-writing must form part of the obituary notice of the twentieth century.

Bertrand Russell

CONTENTS

YOUTH AND OLD AGE

PHILOSOPHY

INTRODUCTION

'I receive on an average 100 letters a day.'

Within his lifetime Bertrand Russell captured the imagination of ordinary people. That lifetime spanned a monumental period, almost one hundred years, from Victorian England to the Space Age. Indeed, Bertrand Russell considered himself something of a Victorian relic—but it is not our intention to regard him as such.

Numerous factors account for the fascination with which the public view Russell. Quite apart from his longevity there are many other roles which made him unique. There is Bertrand Russell the world figure, apostle of peace and champion of humanity; the nonagenarian captivating the youth, inspiring the aged; the aristocrat contemptuous of the House of Lords, and courting imprisonment instead; the controversial political figure, anarchist in temperament, defying the power of the state; the atheist, crossing swords with religious dogma and conventional morality; the mathematician and logician, whose equations destroyed Euclid, yet whose philosophy is comprehensible to the layman. There is also the recipient of the Nobel Prize for Literature, whose elegance of style, incisiveness of irony and wit, harken back to an era when conversation and letters were a cultivated art.

Today, despite an implied failure in the ability of individuals to communicate, the impact Russell made can be measured by the thousands of letters he received from totally unknown persons. Probably no other single great man, and certainly no ordinarily inaccessible philosopher, could ever have had such a prolific and generous exchange of letters with the public.

The purpose of this collection is to give an insight into Bertrand Russell from the viewpoint of the public with whom he corresponded. They have written letters loosely termed 'fan-mail', normally swept aside by researchers as the least valuable section of any great man's collected papers. But Russell was never derisory about correspondence such as this. Amidst the pressure of work and professional commitment, he took the time and trouble to reply, formulating his views precisely, with warmth and humour, irrespective of to whom they were addressed. His response invariably surprised and delighted the recipient.

Among the diverse questions on religion, morals, philosophy and politics, are letters of admiration and support, others hostile and critical, and many simply curious about Russell's personal tastes and habits, his views on youth and old age, and his attitude about the most ordinary things covering a delightful spectrum of his personality.

No newspaper reply columnist has been subject to such an intense onslaught of letters; and these are multi-national in dimension, reflecting Russell's universal appeal. How he was able to cope with this illimitable flow, in conjunction with his writings and his numerous engagements, is explained in reply to a query made in 1963 about his daily routine. Russell answered: '. . . From 8 to 11.30 a.m. I deal with my letters and with the newspapers. I receive on an average 100 letters a day. From 11.30 to 1 p.m. I am seeing people. From 2 to 4 p.m. I read, primarily current nuclear writings. From 4 to 7 p.m. I am writing or seeing people. From 8 to 1 a.m. I am reading and writing.'

Considering that he wrote about seventy books, several thousand articles and essays, was involved in a rich correspondence with the foremost literary, scientific and political figures of our century, like Bernard Shaw, D. H. Lawrence, Joseph Conrad, T. S. Eliot, H. G. Wells, Ludwig Wittgenstein, Schweitzer, Einstein, Nehru and Khrushchev, to name but a few, it is astonishing that he was able to find the time and effort to correspond with thousands of lesser mortals.

On reflection, however, the surprise is bound to subside, for the essential observation about Russell is his concern for the whole of humanity and for each individual. That is why he did not remain detached, but was accessible to the general public, and to the problems raised by anonymous individuals. He crashed through the communication barrier, and the existence of tens of thousands of similar letters to those we have selected, is but proof of the consistent application of his principles.

We have mentioned the various fields of activity in which

Russell excelled. The letters that follow have been categorized accordingly, although it need hardly be said that his ideas and activities were clearly interrelated, resting as they did on an all-embracing desire for truth and the well-being of mankind.

It is estimated from the papers he preserved that Russell wrote one letter every thirty hours of his life. In fact, as he has pointed out, the number was much higher than this, for among other things, 'Whenever I moved house it was usual for quantities of papers to be burned', adding, with characteristic wit, 'Although this all suggests a considerable output, I cannot claim that my pen has been mightier or even busier than other people's swords'.[1]

It is our hope that this selection of letters provides a useful insight into the much examined and discussed life of one of the most extraordinary intellects of our time. If there is anything remaining to be discovered about Bertrand Russell, our claim is to reveal, through his own correspondence, that side of the man which was turned away from the public stage, and directed very much towards each one of us on a personal level. In this respect some might detect an additional role. All the more significant in an age of mass persuasion and closed conformity.

Dating from his fourth marriage in 1952, and thanks to the secretarial assistance given by Lady Russell, there exists what is almost certainly a complete record of Russell's correspondence. There are, for this period alone, some 25,000 exchanges with the general public. The bulk of Russell's correspondents were replied to personally and promptly. In fact, where there had been a delay he invariably apologized. His replies were in most cases brief; a quality partly determined by the pressure of work, but essentially due to an unmatched ability to get to grips with the important points of a letter in a few sentences. A lengthy Russell letter is a rare sight in his archives and it almost always denotes a correspondence about certain complex mathematical or philosophical problems which could not be dealt with in a more concise manner.

[1] From his Preface to *A detailed catalogue of The Archives of Bertrand Russell* (1967).

In preparing this volume it was necessary to considerably abbreviate the incoming letters, retaining only that matter which Russell considered essential when formulating his replies. In a sense this method of editing, though crucial to preserving literary interest and style, may detract from a full awareness of the analytical power of Russell's response: it is an experience to first read one of the many and lengthy letters he received and then to turn to the reply which immediately reveals the salient features of the incoming letter.

On the whole Russell's letters have been kept intact; an occasional sentence has been excised in order to avoid the repetition of opening formalities. The categories we have created are not intended to be precisely definitive of their contents but rather general guides apposite to the great variety of subject-matter dealt with. Within these broad categories we have dispensed with the more orthodox chronological arrangement of letters and have been directed instead by content and continuity of ideas. Similarly footnotes are few and far between; the information that they would carry is served by the biographical data which follows.

BIOGRAPHICAL NOTES

Bertrand Russell was born on May 18, 1872, the son of Lord and Lady Amberley, renowned Victorian radicals, and the grandson of Lord John Russell of Reform Bill fame, who was twice Prime Minister to Victoria. His family tree has roots firmly planted in Whig reformism, beginning with William, Lord Russell who was executed in 1683 for plotting against the Stuarts. At the age of three, both his parents having died, he, together with his older brother Frank, was placed in the care of his grandparents.

Life at his new home was comfortable but cloistered. Russell developed into a shy, lonely boy, dominated by a Spartan (though affectionate) upbringing imposed by his Puritan grandmother. His reserve, no doubt, was further fostered by the mystery of his parents' lives and their early demise; a mystery he was in later years to solve, while editing their private papers. His continuing obsession to find out the truth about life can in part be explained by these early events as can his youthful admiration for his 'godfather' John Stuart Mill and the Utilitarian credo. Russell sought relief from his loneliness by writing, in which he questioned accepted attitudes and beliefs. By early adolescence he was already sceptical of religious dogmas and convinced that human happiness was life's ultimate goal. His undergraduate years at Cambridge, in company with brilliant friends who shared his intense intellectual curiosity, confirmed his genius while breaking down his social reticence. He was transformed into a highly articulate and more outgoing personality.

His first romance led to marriage in 1894, despite vigorous opposition from his family, who steered him into a diplomatic post in Paris in an effort to sever the relationship. Alys Pearsall Smith was a Quaker and an ardent exponent of rights for women. The marriage lasted seventeen years. Russell's preoccupation with his search for a scientific basis to mathematics ended almost at the same time, with the publication in 1910 of the first volume of *Principia Mathematica*. Alys was an undemanding partner, so essential for the concentrated, exacting nature of Russell's work.

Undoubtedly their relationship suited his single-minded dedication.

Although those years were dominated by mathematics there were many diversions and interludes, the most significant of which anticipated Russell's later work and ideas: a period of research into German Socialism, culminating in 1896 in his first published book—an early testament to his interest in human problems; an election campaign fought on behalf of the suffragists in 1907; and, perhaps the most far-reaching, a subjective experience early in 1901 when a friend's illness precipitated 'a mystic insight', bringing into sharp focus Russell's identification with the suffering of others. Not until the outbreak of World War I was this insight to manifest itself in a truly concrete form, in his selfless devotion to the rights of conscientious objectors protesting against the massive slaughterhouse of Europe.

While certain events can be singled out as being of great moment in Russell's life, there are also the very diverse fields to which he applied himself constantly: writing, lecturing, and acting upon many of the important and contentious issues of the day and at the same time making full use of his leisure time to enter into vigorous and sometimes controversial relationships with a host of prominent individuals, including Gilbert Murray, D. H. Lawrence, Ludwig Wittgenstein, Lady Ottoline Morrell and the Bloomsbury Circle, T. S. Eliot and Joseph Conrad. Conrad was one of the few for whom Russell felt a special affinity; a deep empathy despite rare meetings was later marked by Russell naming both his sons after Conrad.

The war impressed a deep social awareness into Russell's thought. Not only did it increase his feelings for the suffering of others, but also through personal privations, including six months' imprisonment, he learnt at first hand of the restrictive powers of the State against which the individual seemed helpless.

In 1920, fired with enthusiasm for the ideals of the Revolution, he visited the Soviet Union in company with a Labour delegation. His reactions to the chaos of the early days of the new soviet state were ambivalent: he welcomed the transformation but was upset by the squalor and suffering he encountered. Having already rejected capitalism he felt that there existed then no happy alternative. He did feel however that guild socialism, which embodies both the principles of common ownership and the sharing of power, elements which he holds as essential to a healthy society, offered the best solution to social problems. His observations on the Russian Revolution were recorded the same year in *The Practice and Theory of Bolshevism*.

On his return from Russia he was offered a visiting lectureship at Peking University and spent nine months in 1920–21 in China, the greater part of it on his back recovering from a succession of serious illnesses. At the time of his illness rumours were circulated that he had died and Russell had the doubtful privilege of reading his own obituary notices. Dora Black was his companion in China and on their return to England they were married.

Russell's early belief in a rational world, nurtured by the confident, self-sufficient Victorian society which was his springboard, was shattered by the war. His disillusionment was completed by his visit to revolutionary Russia. Not that he thought man incapable of rational behaviour: for the next decade he was to attempt to find methods for eliminating the causes of human folly. He was led inevitably into the field of education and, having himself two young children (John Conrad born in 1921 and Katherine in 1923), opened his own school in 1927. He believed that in order to change social thinking there had to be an extensive revision of educational methods and aims. He thought that education should serve international rather than national ends with youth being taught to contest with nature rather than with their fellow men.

The years of family life and his experimental school were very fruitful for Russell's writing. The decade between 1921 and 1931 saw the publication of fifteen books spanning the whole spectrum of social thought and including several aimed specifically at the general public, such as *The ABC of Atoms*, *The ABC of Relativity*, *Marriage and Morals*, and *The Conquest of Happiness*. In addition he contested two elections as an Independent Labour candidate for Chelsea in 1922 and 1923, campaigning among other things for recognition of the Soviet Union. (He was defeated on both occasions.) He found time, too, to undertake four lecture tours of the USA, on the last of which, shortly after his brother's death in

1931, he went as the 3rd Earl Russell. He did not, however, regard the title he had inherited as being important and it was not until 1937 that he made his first speech in the House of Lords. In 1935, after four years of separation, he was divorced from Dora Black. A period of depression and pessimism beginning in 1930 continued. He then returned to work at philosophy, having decided to regain his philosophical reputation.

The advent of National Socialism in Germany brought forth a strong reaction from Russell, who wrote scathingly on the subject. He anticipated a second world war, but in 1936 advocated a pacifist approach to Germany, which he followed up by support of the British Government's Munich policy. He felt that anything was preferable to war and that Germany, faced with no resistance, would recognise the folly of her militarism. After one year of war he was to change this position, having always held that war is sometimes justified when it is indispensable to overpowering a greater evil.

Meanwhile he had married his research secretary, Patricia Spence, and together they edited *The Amberley Papers* published in 1937. In the same year his second son Conrad was born. He and Patricia Russell went to the US with the children following a year later. There he held a succession of professorial posts at universities. In 1940 he was offered a professorship at New York City College but, in that now famous controversy, his appointment was revoked on the grounds of his alleged moral incompatibility with the principles of American education. Thereafter, Russell was boycotted throughout the United States and found himself without any means of livelihood. He was eventually offered a position for five years at the Barnes Foundation, where he lectured on the history of philosophy. Further controversy followed this appointment and he was dismissed after two years. A court case resulted in which Dr Barnes, the head of the Foundation, accused Russell of delivering superficial lectures. The lectures in fact consisted of the first two-thirds of his *History of Western Philosophy*, published in 1945. Russell won the case. In 1944 he returned to England, where he had been appointed a lecturer for five years at and a Life Fellow of Trinity College, Cambridge.

After the atom-bombing of Japan he made one of his rare speeches in the House of Lords predicting the development of the hydrogen bomb and warning of its peril. He had already anticipated the atom bomb as early as 1923 in his book *The ABC of Atoms*. At the end of the war he intensified his campaign for world government. He asserted that the only way to prevent further wars was to vest all power in a supra-national authority. Dissident nations, he maintained, should be forced to subscribe to this authority. Russell felt that similar ideas were embodied in the Baruch proposal, which the US Government accepted. When the USSR rejected them, he suggested that the USSR be threatened with atomic warfare to force her to comply. He felt that his views were further justified by the despotism of Stalin and the seemingly imperialist aims of the USSR. Russell's views at this time heralded a period of unprecedented respectability culminating in many high honours, paramount among which was the Order of Merit in 1949. He did broadcasts for the BBC, lectured to the Armed Forces and was sent as a Government representative to Norway to induce the Norwegians to join in an alliance against the USSR. This period was short-lived, however, for the USSR was soon to develop the atom bomb herself; then Russell became convinced that world peace could only be achieved through joint nuclear disarmament. Also, his unaccustomed respectability caused him to rethink seriously his attitudes. In more recent years he has come to believe that the threat to world peace comes more from the policies of the USA than from those of the USSR. In 1950 Russell travelled first to Australia and then to America as a visiting lecturer. It was while in America that he was told he had been awarded the Nobel Prize for Literature.

A new era in Russell's life began in 1952 with his divorce from Patricia and his marriage to the American writer, Edith Finch. This era is marked by an intensification of his political and creative activities. Where his outlook in the 1930s and during the turbulent years of the war was bleak and pessimistic, his innate optimism and faith in humanity were rapidly regenerated during the 1950s.

His major concern now was to work to prevent nuclear war. Faced with a formidable assembly of areas of activity, he first concentrated his fire on the increase of illiberalism in America which reached its zenith during the McCarthyist period. Russell had always championed the cause of persecuted persons, believing as he does in the supremacy of the individual. In 1916 six conscientious objectors were imprisoned for distributing a pacifist leaflet, whereupon Russell declared himself to be the author, inviting the authorities to take action against him instead. The result was a trial famous for Russell's defence. He was fined £100 and then summarily dismissed from his post at Trinity College. The transcript of his defence was later published, only to be banned by the government. His record of successful intervention on behalf of political prisoners is impressive. One colourful example is Rákosi, the famous Hungarian communist imprisoned by the Horthyists, who owed much to Russell's plea which eventually led to his release in 1940 in exchange for Hungarian flags captured by the Russians in 1849.

Russell was shocked by the sentence passed on the Rosenbergs and their subsequent execution in 1953. He quickly took up the cudgels on behalf of Morton Sobell, who was accused of complicity with the Rosenbergs and imprisoned. Later, during the 'sixties, Russell was to campaign for countless individuals, Ben Barka, Tony Ambatielos and Heinz Brandt prominent among these, and also to sponsor an investigation into the assassination of President Kennedy.

With his increasing commitment to the anti-war cause his name became synonymous with peace campaigns. His home was flooded with letters from all over the world. Answering these added extra work to an already full agenda.

In 1954 the Bikini hydrogen bomb tests emphasized the urgency of his task. His 'Man's Peril' broadcast on the BBC struck hard at public apathy by bringing home the full consequences of nuclear war. In an effort to create an influential platform for nuclear disarmament he spent the next three years recruiting major scientists from all over the world who were sympathetic to his aims. A manifesto was prepared which was signed initially by Einstein shortly before his death. The signatories to this document formed the nucleus of the First Pugwash Conference of Scientists from both East and West, held in Nova Scotia in 1957.

Russell was elected president of that and succeeding conferences. The Pugwash Movement in aim and achievement brought to government and public attention the increasing hazards to human life due to the development of nuclear weapons. Its most noteworthy achievement was its role in the partial test-ban treaty concluded in 1963. Russell, however, was not satisfied that Pugwash could wield decisive influence towards disarmament. He therefore turned determinedly to other methods. In 1916 he had written an open letter to Woodrow Wilson appealing to him to help stop the war. In the same spirit he now wrote to Eisenhower and Khrushchev urging rapprochement between their Governments. Dulles replied on behalf of Eisenhower and the ensuing correspondence, though serving only to confirm each government's position, when published in book form in 1958 (*The Vital Letters of Russell, Khrushchev, Dulles*) brought to public notice more clearly than ever before the respective attitudes of the great powers towards disarmament. This correspondence foreshadowed the hundreds of letters Russell was to write to leaders all over the world bearing directly upon urgent issues of the day.

Not content with the response so far elicited, he turned with boundless energy to the possibility of averting war through mass protest. 1958 saw the launching of the Campaign for Nuclear Disarmament with Russell as president. Four years of intense activity followed, with Russell, now firmly established as the apostle of peace, first leading massive protest marches, and then, through the Committee of 100, mass civil disobedience in an attempt to meet effectively the increasing threat of nuclear war. In 1961, shortly after leading a sit-down outside the Ministry of Defence, he and his wife were arrested and imprisoned.

Although his activities during this period ran counter to the policies of the Western powers, his multitude of achievements and dedication to the future of humanity continued to exact formal recognition from many social organizations. In 1957 he was awarded the Kalinga Prize by UNESCO for his major part in popularizing science. Denmark awarded him the Sonning Prize in 1960 for his contribution to the advancement of European culture. The year he was jailed, he was elected Honorary Fellow of the London School of Economics and, in May 1962, on his ninetieth birthday, a luncheon was given in his honour at the House of Commons.

Despite his age and overwhelming commitments, his writing flourished. Not the least of his achievements since 1952 was the publication of twenty books and several hundred articles, constituting almost one-third of his life's output. Included are his first books of short stories, *Satan in the Suburbs* and *Nightmares of Eminent Persons*, and several important philosophical and ethical works, such as *Human Society in Ethics and Politics*, *My Philosophical Development*, and *Why I am Not a Christian*.

His method of direct contact with world leaders was completely vindicated in 1962 when Russell appealed for compromise to Khrushchev and Kennedy during the Cuban crisis and to Nehru and Chou En-lai over the Sino-Indian border conflict. The mutual respect built up in a lengthy correspondence before as well as during this period, especially with Nehru and Khrushchev, undoubtedly influenced the course of events. An account of the events together with the correspondence was published the following year in *Unarmed Victory*.

By 1963 his total involvement had increased to such an extent that the Bertrand Russell Peace Foundation was formed, an organization designed to lift some of the burden of work off Russell's shoulders as well as to consolidate the wide support he had won. The Foundation is concerned mainly with international problems, especially support for the aspirations of the people in countries of the 'third world'. Russell consistently abhorred colonialism and defended the rights of national liberation movements. After his visit to China in 1921 he supported the Chinese in their efforts to liberate themselves from foreign control. At the same time he wrote articles warning against the increasing world influence of American finance. He was critical too of British imperial policy: in 1901 censuring Britain's role in South Africa, in the 'thirties her role in India, and in more recent years deploring her tacit support of apartheid policies in South Africa and in Rhodesia.

Since 1963 he devoted much of his attention to the war in Vietnam, fiercely condemning American involvement. Because of the British Government's support for American policies he resigned from the British Labour Party in 1965. A year later he addressed the preparatory meeting of the International War Crimes Tribunal set up to investigate actions committed by the Americans in Vietnam. Russell was elected president of the Tribunal, whose first findings were published in 1967, as was Russell's *War Crimes in Vietnam*. The full record of the Tribunal is published in *Against the Crime of Silence* (1968). The London demonstrations in the spring of 1968 against the Vietnam War, organized by the Vietnam Solidarity Campaign, were due in no small part to Russell, for in 1966 he had been instrumental in setting up the Campaign and made a speech to its founding conference.

Between 1967 and 1969 the three volumes of his Autobiography appeared and received wide acclaim. Russell's last public act was a statement on the Middle East crisis which was read, on his behalf, to the World Congress of Parliamentarians in Cairo on February 3, 1970, the day after his death.

No 2. Lane 26 Chung Cheng Road
Tansui, Formosa
Jan 21. 1963.

Lord Bertrand Russell
England.

Dear Lord Russell:
How are you Lord Russell ?

Sincerely yours
Frederick F. Lin

January 31, 1963

Dear Mr Lin,
  Thank you for your letter. I am fine. I am struggling against nuclear warfare which I feel is important. I hope you are well also.
  With good wishes,—and thanks for your photo.
Yours sincerely
Bertrand Russell

31

MOST, 24th June 1962.

Dear Sir !

Sorry our imperfection of Letter. We not know
English. - We consul a the Dictionary.

We are young mans /19 year/. Great impressive
on our make your the assays, which emanate in
Czechoslovakia.
We like your the philosophy.
Especially hawe we like your Atheism the stand-
point.
Veri we appreciate your Activity for the good
peace.
Besides we admire your of Politics no-compromise.
Sorry we no be issued more your Books in Czech.

Wish you we plenty of Force in further the Activity and of Life !

Good-by ,

Citizen's of Czechoslovakia, Josef D i n d a
and Jiří R a d a .

July 27, 1962

Dear Mr Dinda and Mr Rada,

Thank you very much for your letter of the 24th June. Please accept my apologies for not having replied to you before. I am extremely grateful to you for the kind things you have had to say about me, and your encouragement for my work for nuclear disarmament. I very much hope that people such as yourself in Czechoslovakia will press constantly for solutions of the problems of the nuclear age, despite the difficulties you undoubtedly encounter.

I enclose a copy of the statement I gave to the Moscow Disarmament Congress.

With best wishes,

Yours sincerely
Bertrand Russell

232 Woodstock Rd
Oxford
10-11-61
Dear Mr Bertrand
Russell,
Thank you very much
for all the things you
have done.
I like you.

If you come to Oxford
come and have tea
with me
Love from
Paul Altmann
I am six years old

November 24, 1961

Dear Paul Altmann,

Thank you for your very nice letter which I am especially glad to have because it encourages me to keep on working. I wish that I could have tea with you but I do not expect to come to Oxford. If I do come, I will let you know.

With love and warmest good wishes

from
Bertrand Russell

DEAR BERTRAND RUSSELL . . .

HOSEI UNIVERSITY
FUJIMICHO CHIYODA-KU,
TOKYO, JAPAN.

TELEPHONE:
TOKYO (301) 2351

Sept. 15, 1961.

Lord Bertrand Russell,
London.

My Lord:

We are informed by Tokyo papers that Lord and Lady Russell were sentenced to seven days in jail for declining to abandon plans for a sit-down protest against nuclear weapons.

We believe that all the peace-loving people of the world were deeply impressed by your dauntless attitude for world peace and were much encouraged by the fact that you preferred prison to discarding your belief, and we are just one of many such people.

We sincerely hope the unreasonable imprisonment will never injure your health and that you will carry on, together with your friends all over the world, your campaign for total disarmament against nuclear weapons.

Very respectfully yours,

Prof. Hideomi Tuge.

Prof. N. Funahashi.

Prof. Hiroshi Hasegawa.

Prof. Tadashi Nakajima.

Prof. Fumio Kurahashi.

Prof. Kiyoji Honda.

Prof. Soya Aoki.

Prof. Geoju Akita.

Prof. Shizuo Komobuchi.

Prof. Komaki Omi.

36

RELIGION

FOREWORD

*'I am not a Christian, and have not been a Christian
since the age of fifteen.'*

Throughout his life Bertrand Russell opposed religion and
rejected the idea of a supreme being—views, need it be said,
which have never ceased to provoke the orthodox. Indeed, the
radical views of his free-thinking parents, Lord and Lady
Amberley, were considered outrageous by the Victorian society
of their day. Not that Russell was to be given the advantages of
this somewhat disrespectful environment. The Amberleys died
very young, and although they had wished that Bertrand and his
elder brother be placed under the guardianship of two atheist
friends, the will was set aside by a court order, and the boys
were placed in the care of their grandparents.

Bertrand Russell described those formative years as follows:
'My grandfather, the statesman, died in 1878, and it was his
widow who decided the manner of my education. She was a
Scotch Presbyterian, who gradually became a Unitarian. I was
taken on alternate Sundays to the Parish Church and to the
Presbyterian Church, while at home I was taught the tenets of
Unitarianism. Eternal punishment and the literal truth of the
Bible were not inculcated, and there was no Sabbatarianism
beyond a suggestion of avoiding cards on Sunday for fear of
shocking the servants. But in other respects morals were austere,
and it was held to be certain that conscience, which is the voice of
God, is an infallible guide in all practical perplexities.'[1] The result
was not quite what his grandmother may have wished, though
perhaps it might have been predicted that, given the same childhood régime, Russell was soon to develop an outlook not unlike
that of his father. At the age of fifteen, to avoid detection, he was
recording his religious doubts in Greek letters in a book he headed
'Greek Exercises'. By the time he was eighteen, shortly before
going up to Cambridge, he had abandoned all uncertainty, be-

[1] From 'My Religious Reminiscences' reprinted in *The Basic Writings
of Bertrand Russell.*

39

come an atheist, and was later to recall in his Autobiography: 'Throughout the long period of religious doubt, I had been rendered very unhappy by the gradual loss of belief, but when the process was completed, I found to my surprise that I was quite glad to be done with the whole subject.'

The isolation of his youth ended in the liberation he found at Cambridge in the 1890s. Russell undoubtedly revelled in the atmosphere of those days and as late as 1961 was to recollect one of his contemporaries as follows: 'I knew Ralph Vaughan Williams well when he was an undergraduate . . . [he] was in those days a most determined atheist and was noted for having walked into Hall one day saying in a loud voice, "Who believes in God now-a-days, I should like to know?" '

But it was no mere whim to shock the devout that drove Russell to oppose religious dogma, for he considered all the great religions of the world not only untrue, but harmful. 'It is evident as a matter of logic, that since they disagree, not more than one of them can be true', he has written in 'My Religious Reminiscences', and further, 'The question of the truth of a religion is one thing, but the question of its usefulness is another. I am as firmly convinced that religions do harm as I am that they are untrue.'

That Bertrand Russell enjoyed demolishing the sacred cows of religious orthodoxy, whether they be Hindu or any other variety, is apparent from the following selection of letters. But underlying them all, clearly to be seen, is his deep sympathy and concern for the feelings of his fellow humans; his desire that they should be freed from the harmful shackles of dogma and superstition and his firm opposition to false beliefs with their undesirable social consequences.

'. . . would you call yourself a Christian at the moment. A brief, just negative or affirmative, answer would be quite sufficient; I wish only to end a tiresome and lengthy dispute—which also engenders much hard feeling. . . .'

December 28, 1961

Dear Mr Salmon,

Thank you for your letter. I should like to make clear that I am not a Christian, and have not been a Christian since the age of fifteen. Throughout my life I have made every effort to let it be known that I am not a Christian, and why I am not a Christian. I hope that this will settle your argument: it is not a question about which there has ever been ground for dispute.

Yours sincerely
Bertrand Russell

'I am at the moment engaged in a dispute with a Mr. Joseph Lewis, an ardent atheist . . . as to exactly what your views are on the subject of atheism. Mr. Lewis insists that you endorse the matter beyond any doubt, whereas I feel, from reading your books which emphasize skepticism and which deplore faith, that you are instead an agnostic. . . .'

March 18, 1958

Dear Mr Major,

Thank you for your letter of March 9. I do not wonder that you and Mr. Lewis are in doubt as to whether to call me an atheist or an agnostic as I am myself in doubt upon this point and call myself sometimes the one and sometimes the other. I think that in philosophical strictness at the level where one doubts the existence of material objects and holds that the world may have existed for only five minutes, I ought to call myself an agnostic; but, for all practical purposes, I am an atheist. I do not think the existence of the Christian God any more probable that the existence of the Gods of Olympus or Valhalla. To take another illustration: nobody can prove that there is not between the

41

Earth and Mars a china teapot revolving in an elliptic orbit, but nobody thinks this sufficiently likely to be taken into account in practice. I think the Christian God just as unlikely.

Yours sincerely
Bertrand Russell

'. . . Many years ago I had a chance meeting with a religious confrere of mine who had spent some time in China . . . and was there when you were on a lecture trip. It seems, as I recall the story, that you fell ill and spent a long time in a missionary hospital in China—your condition most critical . . . when you were beginning to make progress you talked with great penitence with your Missionary nurse expressing the question whether she thought God would ever or could ever forgive you for the way you had ripped down students' religious faith all over the Orient. . . .'

November 24, 1950

Dear Mr Lippincott,

Thank you for your letter. I am interested at the recrudescence of an entirely fictitious story which began in 1921 and which I had supposed had died down by this time.

In that year I had double pneumonia in Peking and only one English nurse was obtainable. She was a lady of great piety who told me when I was convalescent that she had had great struggles with her conscience on the ground that she thought it her duty to let me die, although professional instinct proved too strong for this virtuous impulse. I was delirious for a fortnight and as soon as the delirium ended I had no recollection whatever of the two weeks that had passed. During these two weeks the aforesaid nurse looked after me at night and my wife looked after me by day. It appears that when I coughed I was in the habit of lapsing into profanity in ways which the nurse mistook for serious appeals to the Deity. This, at least, was what my wife told me. The hospital by-the-way was not a Missionary Hospital, it was a German Hospital, nor was the nurse a Missionary Nurse.

42

Stories of this sort are always spread about Unbelievers. You may have noticed that when Shaw became unconscious shortly before his death the local Anglican Parson rushed round knowing that Shaw was no longer in a position to turn him out and pretended to the world that Shaw had made a pious and edifying end.

Yours sincerely
Bertrand Russell

'. . . Buddha boldly turned atheist but the inventors of other religions did not do so. We cannot say they did not have sufficient courage to declare it. They were the rebellious minds of their ages. . . . Moreover if the teachings of all of them are taken in the very broadest sense their message is the same "Believe in One Supreme Reality and do good deeds." Why did such a strange coincidence occur? . . .'

May 13, 1962

Dear Miss Nasira,

Thank you very much for your letter. You are quite right that Buddha did not wish his ideas to be reduced to an arid orthodoxy with an autocratic priesthood, but I think that he is exceptional in this respect. It may be true that many religious teachers in past millennia have sought what they considered to be a supreme reality, but most of them expressed this in terms of a personality which they conceived to have the powers over men that no doubt they felt their fathers to have had when they were small children.

I think the problem which you wish me to solve can be answered in this way. Men find the world a difficult place, and in many ways frightening. They feel that they cannot cope with their problems, and that they cannot face their fear of being alone in a hostile environment, with the possibility of accident, sickness, death and misfortune. As a result, they invent powerful figures whom they name gods. I agree that this lacks courage, and although it is true that many religious leaders who have believed in a deity have had a kind of personal courage in the face of persecution, I believe that they lacked the intellectual courage to face the

43

world without the comfort of such a myth. For in the final analysis, it is human responsibility which is significant in our affairs. I should be very happy if you would read my book *Why I am Not a Christian*, in which I have included an essay called 'A Free Man's Worship'; in this I explain my position fully.

Thank you for your interesting letter.

Yours sincerely
Bertrand Russell

'. . . The title of *Why I am Not a Christian* intrigues me, because your whole attitude on the TV (Brains Trust) seemed to me, in its gentleness and tolerance, its humour, and its desire for an impartial knowledge and expression of the truth, so utterly and profoundly Christian. . . . The fact seems to be that our conceptions of what Christianity is seems to be very different. My own approach from my youth up, was never standard Anglican in the mid-Victorian sense, and was always very unlike that of Boughey and Blenkin. You see I owed the best part of my education to a lay Headmaster (Scotch) who was a distinguished chemist, a former Fellow of Johns, and one who accepted all the best new critical views of the Bible. I therefore never had anything to unlearn, but started *ab initio* as a Modernist Christian. My best and most intimate school friend was a Presbyterian, and my parish priest an Irish Anglo-Catholic. So I always tended to have an eclectic way of looking at things. . . .'

October 13, 1957

Dear Dr Bouquet,

Thank you for your letter of October 7. It is true that our conceptions of what Christianity is are very different. You judge it from your friends; I judge it from its impact on social life through the Churches. If you care to read the account of my troubles in New York in 1940 (at the end of my book *Why I am Not a Christian*) or the outbursts of savagery against Mrs. Knight's broadcasts (some of the less offensive of which were published in the *Listener*), you will I think be compelled to admit

44

that in the West influential persons calling themselves Christians have almost a monopoly of intolerance. I consider the official Catholic attitude on divorce, birth control, and censorship exceedingly dangerous to mankind. General Franco, whom Sir Winston Churchill praised as a 'gallant Christian Gentleman', has forbidden any work of fiction alluding to adultery, though I believe he had made a special exception for the Iliad. The virtues which you would consider specifically Christian, are thought in Japan to be specifically Buddhist and in India to be specifically Hindu. I consider all these claims unfounded. It is in the name of kindliness and tolerance that I oppose organized creeds, Christian, Eastern and Communist, all alike. I do not think the existence of kindly individuals in organizations which are as a whole intolerant is a reason for not opposing such organizations.

Yours sincerely
Bertrand Russell

'I "observed" the New Year's Eve television programme in which you were arraigned before those questioners as if by the Inquisition itself. It must have been an ordeal. . . . But, if I may say so, you did say some extraordinary things, even if not all of them seriously. . . . Is it not, for example, a gross error to say that there have not been many believers, persons with firm Christian faith, who have done much to promote every kindness, tolerance and the good of others in many ways? . . . a service directly inspired by the "dogmatic" faith that they accept. I am also surprised that you brush aside so easily the possibility of there being any truth in religious faith. Was it not your generation which put the matter to the test more thoroughly, so far as historical enquiry goes, than ever before? A balanced judgement of its findings would, I maintain, be that, while the original conclusions of the critics were too extreme and cannot now be sustained, progress was made in two ways. Superstition and unnecessary beliefs, were in many ways eradicated. . . . Philosophically also there have been gains. The inadequate theist arguments have been given heavy punishment, but certain firm lines have been

45

strengthened under the test. I mean such methods as were practised by Augustine and Aquinas and which the modern Monists
are attempting to develop to meet new problems. . . . I don't
accuse you of malice, but of, at least, oversight. You did not speak
your mind in relation to realities, the achievements of half a
century of work by philosophers, theologians and historians. . . .
I am writing because you seem to me to be a man who influences
the average citizen and in some respects towards error and dogma-
tism, a direction you yourself wish no one to take. . . . I don't
know what exactly the Queen meant by the "splendid beliefs" of
our ancestors but I think some of them are common ground for
most of us. Would you disagree? If you are not displeased by this
letter, meant in good spirit, please accept my sincere good wishes.'

January 3, 1953

Dear Father Holdsworth,

Thank you for your letter. I will admit at once that the people
with whom I was arguing irritated me and that, the time being
short, I made statements that were more slap-dash and unquali-
fied than they would have been if I had had more leisure and less
provocation. I do not of course deny that a very great many
Christians have been filled with humane feelings and have lived
heroic lives with a view to mitigating suffering. What I think on
the other side, and what of course makes an unbridgeable disagreement between you and me, is that even these men, in so far
as their activities redounded to the credit of the Church as an in-
stitution, unintentionally and unwittingly did more harm than
good. People are apt to speak as if the Church throughout history
had been kindly and had shown some respect for the outlook of
its Founder, but if you will ask yourself by what process the
cruelties of the Middle Ages have been mitigated—for example
the burning of heretics and witches—you will find that the
protagonists in every campaign for mercy have been inorthodox.
The Church as long as it dared impeded the progress of medicine
by frowning on dissection. The Church was so shocked by geology
that the Sorbonne condemned Buffon for maintaining that some
present-day mountains are not as old as the world. The Church in
recent years has been softening its doctrines on eternal damna-

tion, but it has done so entirely owing to attacks from the inorthodox. In the present day, the opposition of the Church to birth
control, if it could be successful, would mean that poverty and
starvation must forever be the lot of mankind unless alleviation
is brought by the hydrogen bomb.

These are some of the reasons which make me think the Church
harmful. The reasons which make me think its doctrines untrue
are of course totally different, since we cannot know *a priori* either
that truth is useful or that error is harmful.

The latter part of your letter is concerned with the intellectual
arguments. I do not myself feel that any of the modern re-
statements of the old arguments for the existence of God are any
improvement. I do not think there is a single one of them which
would carry conviction except to one who ardently desired the
truth of their conclusion. You speak of 'the achievement of half
a century of work by philosophers, theologians and historians.' I
do not quite know what you have in mind. There are many schools
of philosophers and, since Constantine, most Western philosophers have accepted Christian dogma. At most times and in most
places throughout Christendom they could not otherwise have
done their work unimpeded or earned a living wage. Historians
also are much divided. Ever since 1917 they have been so terrified
of or attracted by Bolshevism that few of them have been able
to think straight.

I have said all these things dogmatically because it would take a
lot of space to say them in any other way, but I agree of course
that what I have been saying is controversial. You ask about the
'splendid beliefs' of which the Queen spoke. Frankly I think this
is pernicious rubbish. The beliefs of our ancestors included the
belief that men should be burnt alive at the stake, that traitors
should be hanged, drawn and quartered, that torture should be
used in criminal proceedings, and that sturdy vagabonds should
be branded. I fail to see anything 'splendid' in these beliefs.
There were of course better beliefs than these that some men
held at some times. I think there is much to be said for Algernon
Sidney and Thomas Jefferson, of whom we killed the first and
tried to kill the second. But by and large I think the prevailing
beliefs of past times were both cruel and ignorant.

Your letter did not in any way displease me, and I wish I might hope that mine will not have displeased you.

Yours sincerely
Bertrand Russell

'. . . I am sixteen and in my last year at High school I have just finished reading your book, *Why I am Not a Christian* and I am very impressed by it. . . . Last week I was talking with the headmaster and he said that he believed that religion is responsible for our moral code. I disagree with him since this leaves the implication that all atheists and agnostics are immoral. . . .'

April 27, 1966

Dear Mr Walker,
. . . It is probably true that religion is responsible for our moral code, or at least for a moral code. This moral code had its basis in the Bible but was then formalised by people who wanted to suppress all those things of which they were most afraid.

By some people's standards I suppose that atheists and agnostics might be considered immoral in the eyes of a professed Christian. However even Christians are not without blemish. They have been guilty of:
  1. Torture in the Congo.
  2. The condemnation of Dreyfus.
  3. Continued support of nuclear warfare.
I could continue this list for ever but it seems enough to put them in bad odour from a moral point of view.

Yours sincerely
Bertrand Russell

'. . . one thing continues to puzzle me: the world into which science is leading us bears an ever-increasing resemblance to that envisioned by the ancient theologies . . . could the so-called primitives have arrived by sheer guess-work at the true nature of the cosmos. . . .'

48

October 22, 1962

Dear Mr Curtis,

Thank you very much for your letter. I am afraid that I do not agree that contemporary events bear out scriptural prophecy except in the sense that virtually anything can be so considered if the inclination to do so exists. My own preference is to look upon theological writings as the slightly historical fantasy world of primitive tribesmen, often savage and sometimes of interest.

Yours sincerely
Bertrand Russell

'. . . In reply to the question, "How does an Agnostic regard the Bible?", you impute to all Christians, except those whom you label "the enlightened clerics", a narrow interpretation of it, . . . You are badly misinformed if you think that many Christians would not agree with your comments on Elisha, the jeering children, and the she-bears. . . . The Anglican Communion (amongst others) does not require its adherents to hold either your views of the Bible or the fundamentalist views which you use as an example. . . .'

June 16, 1960

Dear Mr Lord,

. . . Your remarks to the effect that Christians for the most part do not believe in the Bible do not seem to me quite valid. You say, for example, that the Anglican Communion does not demand a fundamentalist attitude to the Bible. You do not seem to know that in the service for the Ordering of Deacons the Bishop says: 'Do you unfeignedly believe all the Canonical Scriptures of the Old and New Testament?' And the Ordinand has to answer: 'I do believe them.' You will say, no doubt, that this does not matter, since no one expects a parson to speak the truth about important matters on solemn occasions. But, for my part, I think it a pity that people who are intended to stand for virtue have to begin their career by a solemn lie.

Furthermore, while, in fact, as you say, most priests do not believe those parts of the Bible which they find inconvenient, many of them do believe some texts which they consider justifications for inflicting great pain and hardship: for example, those forbidding divorce and birth control. Most of them reject the pacifism recommended in the Sermon of the Mount, but accept with glee the text in which Christ says that he has come to bring, not peace, but a sword. . . .

Yours sincerely
Bertrand Russell

'I am engaged in research on . . . Bishop Charles Gore, and should be . . . grateful . . . if you would give me some information about the public debate between Bishop Gore and yourself which took place in the Great Hall, University College, London, in 1928. . . .'[1]

November 13, 1958

Dear Mr Carpenter,
I am sorry to say that I have no recollection of the impression made upon me by Bishop Gore on the occasion to which you allude. The only thing that I remember about the occasion is that it occurred when my son, then aged six, was suffering intolerable pain from mastoid for which he was about to be operated, and that one of Bishop Gore's supporters in the debate maintained that all pain is a punishment for sin.

Yours sincerely
Bertrand Russell

'I am writing to you for help with a problem that is torturing me terribly. . . . I have not accepted the Christian faith since I was about 20 years old. . . . A fortnight ago someone lent me a

[1] The debate was entitled 'Are the claims of Christianity valid?' and took place on February 12, 1929.

book called *Mere Christianity* by a man called C. S. Lewis . . . he says the only way to gain eternal life is to give your life to Christ. Throw your life away blindly, he says; there must be a real death of your own personality, death of your dearest ambitions, death of your dearest wishes. It made me feel that if I didn't leave my babies and go nursing sick natives or something like that I would go to Hell. . . . I have been so distressed and I have had no one to tell it to. My husband is very good but his main interests in life are football and television. . . .

April 26, 1958

Dear Madam,

Thank you for your letter which I have read with great interest and much sympathy. I think you have allowed yourself to be impressed more than is necessary by C. S. Lewis. The whole idea of throwing away your life blindly as an imagined service to Christ is a form of glorifying masochism and of self-abasement before power. It is the same pattern as that of the Russians who made confessions of guilt when prosecuted by Stalin. It is an essentially oriental attitude which Christianity took over when it attributed to God the moral defects of cruel despots.

You would be doing a completely wrong act if you abandoned your children in order to practise some spectacular self-sacrifice in a distant country. You should try to bear in mind that there is no reason to believe in Christian doctrines and that much of the Christian ethic is unworthy of self-respecting people. You will find this sort of thing said at greater length in my recent book *Why I am Not a Christian*. I have every wish to bring you comfort and reassurance, and I should be glad to know whether you make progress in this direction.

Yours sincerely
Bertrand Russell

'. . . in order to marry the girl I love, and who loves me, I have to persuade her to give up her Catholicism and become an atheist or agnostic . . . for purely tactical reasons, I find myself giving or withholding my affection—promising not to kiss her for a week, because she pleads that this kind of sin keeps her away from the sacraments, then leading her on by my coldness until she yields and asks me to spend the night with her, and finally getting her to admit that she cannot possibly feel that what she has done is wrong. I am not sure whether this conduct is defensible—I dare say it is—but I cannot help hating it . . . she has made me agree to meet a priest she knows and argue with him. . . .'

September 6, 1960

Dear Sir,

. . . I have every sympathy with your wish to convert your fiancée to free thought and I hope you will succeed. I think however, that you should exercise some caution as regards sexual blackmail for, if not, her priest may tell her that you, with the help of Satan, are enlisting the lusts of the flesh to tempt her along the primrose path; and there is a chance that she may believe him. I think, if I were in your place, I should confine myself to arguments having more logical cogency, difficult as this may be.

Yours sincerely
Bertrand Russell

———

'. . . The nature of religion as a superstitious paralyser of thought . . . seems self-evident . . . however, there is a doubt in my mind as to the proper attitude in various cases: The sincere belief of the old lady that she will meet again her dead husband sustains her in her later years. . . . The child who fears the dark is consoled by the reassurance that Jesus is watching over her. . . . The ill person who apparently survives and grows well through persistent religious faith is another example . . . under these conditions it may be desirable to foster the faith which is present. . . .'

December 3, 1959

Dear Mr Simons,

Thank you for your letter. I should not myself attempt to upset the faith of an elderly lady who believed in the life after death.

But, from a public point of view, there are more important considerations: 1. If it is thought desirable that certain beliefs should be supported without regard to evidence as to their truth, one is landed with censorship and all its evils. 2. The great majority of false beliefs have undesirable social consequences—e.g., Catholics oppose birth control and Anglicans oppose the marriage of divorced persons. 3. The attitude of seeking comfort through false beliefs is somewhat ignoble. 4. The question of children is more difficult than that of old people because one has to consider their future social activities. On the whole, I do not think it a good plan to comfort children by lies. I think sympathy without lies is better.

Yours sincerely
Bertrand Russell

'. . . Forty years ago it seemed inevitable that the victory of Science at the end of its fifty year battle with Religion would lead to an increase in rationality; has not this hope been largely disappointed? It seems to me that, except in a few highly civilised places, the defeat of dogmatic Christianity has only caused people to embrace newer and cruder theologies. Christianity, simple because it is old, has been much refined and even liberalised during the centuries. . . . If religion is something that a large part of mankind cannot or will not (at present) do without, then an old and mellow religion must be preferred to a new and brash one. . . .'

January 10, 1953

Dear Mr Barwise,

. . . I am to a very great extent in agreement with the views that you express. I have been saying for the last thirty years that the ultimate contest will be between the Vatican, and the Kremlin, and that in that contest I shall side with the Vatican. My ground for preferring the Vatican is the same as yours, viz.: that religions, like wines, mature with age. I should on this ground prefer Buddhism to Christianity if it were a practical alternative, but I should desert logic if asked to back fetichism. I do not think that either the Nazi or the Communist religion embodies the religious needs of populations. I think both express merely the will to power of governments, and the incapacity of subjects to stand up against modern governmental techniques.

Yours sincerely
Bertrand Russell

'. . . My husband and I do not attend any church and consider ourselves agnostics. We do, however, feel that a religious education of some kind is desirable for our children, our feeling being that when they are grown, they can decide for themselves. . . .'

December 2, 1964

Dear Mrs Nofer,
. . . I frequently receive letters from America asking the same questions as you put to me. In a bigoted community such questions are not very easy to answer. I think, on the whole, it is better for your children, while in school, to conform tacitly to whatever is generally practised in the way of religion, but I do not consider that you should conceal your own view from them. I think a child has a just grievance if, when he or she grows up, parents are found to have lied about religion. I do not agree that some kind of religious education is essential. I think that all religions consist at least in part of believing things for which there is no evidence and I think that in face of such beliefs loyalty to evidence should be substituted. You may consider that it is bad for a child to have one set of beliefs instilled at home and another at school, but I think the harm done by any other cause is greater.

Yours sincerely
Bertrand Russell

'I have been disturbed for some time about the disproportionate growth of the Roman Catholic Church in the United States . . .

54

[which] is straining every nerve in order to overwhelm any rivals through sheer force of numbers. . . . In my opinion this is the same as the provoking of an armament race. Therefore, I would very much like to see the non-Catholic peoples of the west . . . match the Catholics in this respect. . . .'

March 21, 1958

Dear Mr Rasmussen,

The subject about which you write in your letter of March 10 is one which has occupied my mind off and on for the last fifty years. I do not like your suggestion that non-Catholics should copy the Catholics in excessive breeding. This is exactly analogous to the piling up of competitive armaments. I think the better way is to try to liberalize Catholic populations. I believe statistics prove that, in spite of the priests, the birthrate among Catholics has seriously declined in America. The Church has shown some softening in its opposition to family limitation, particularly in sanctioning the confining of intercourse to the 'safe period'. I think it is wiser to work to improve Catholic practice than to urge that non-Catholic practice should deteriorate.

Yours sincerely
Bertrand Russell

'. . . My husband and I are both agnostics. Could you advise me on whether or not to have a child baptised in the Christian faith and bring him up as a Christian when the parents are not Christians. . . .'

December 10, 1959

Dear Mrs Hughes,

I hardly know what to say to you about how an agnostic should bring up children who will have to live in a Christian country. I did not have my own children baptised and let them know my own attitude towards religion. The result was not exactly as I should have wished. Two of them have become earnest Anglicans. I do not think one should conceal one's attitude on theological questions, but I am not at all sure that one should take any positive steps to keep them inorthodox. I am sorry not to have anything more definite to say to you, but I think the answer should differ according to the environment in which the child will probably live.

Yours sincerely
Bertrand Russell

'During a Television interview you quoted a member of the Episcopate of the Anglican Church. I understood you to say that this Bishop felt that some of your views were occasioned by "sexual lust". I cannot believe it. This must have been a very young bishop. . . . I can only add that I have more than once deplored the fact that you, yourself, were not a Bishop. . . .'

March 29, 1961

Dear Canon Coleman,
    Thank you for your friendly letter of February 23. The Bishop in question was not a young man. He was the late Bishop of Rochester (England). I omitted to ask him what passages in *Principia Mathematica* gave evidence of sexual lust. It is kind of you to say that you wish I were a bishop, but I cannot pretend to feel any great regret on this account.

Yours sincerely
Bertrand Russell

'I enclose a copy of *Waarom Ek Geen Christen is Nie*. . . . We have printed 3000 copies and hope to dispose of them before fresh legislation, imposing an internal censorship is passed. . . .'

February 21, 1960

Dear Mr Roux,
    Thank you for sending me the translation of *Why I am Not a Christian* and for your kind letter. I suppose that, as you say, the

56

translation will shortly be suppressed.[1] The South African Government seems to be bent on demonstrating all that I have to say against Christianity by proving itself the most zealously Christian Government in the world.

Yours sincerely
Bertrand Russell

'... In *Wisdom of the West* the picture of the Prophet of Islam has been cut from the copies of the book supplied to Pakistan ... its publication is tabooed in Islam. ... I wonder where was the occasion for publishing the picture of the Holy Prophet in a book, entitled, *Wisdom of the West*? In your book you have used the word "Flight" for the migration of the Holy Prophet from Mecca to Medina. ... "Hijrat" (migration) was a strategic withdrawal to a friendly place made according to plan, under Divine guidance. You will not like to use the word "flight" when the British armies took to their heels at Dunkirk in World War II. How do you account for using the word "flight" for an event that has a religious sanctity for the Muslim world? Sir, I wonder how you can undo the wrong that you have done to the Muslim world. ...'

September 16, 1963

Dear Mr Irshad,

Thank you for your letter. 1. The British armies did flee from Dunkirk just as Mohammed *fled* from Mecca to Medina. 2. I do not believe that Mohammed or anyone else was impelled by 'divine inspiration'. 3. To call flight 'strategic withdrawal' is ludicrous. 4. The picture of the prophet should be displayed as a matter of interest to students and scholars. 5. Chauvinism is harmful and also accompanies the absence of any humour or humility.

Yours sincerely
Bertrand Russell

P.S. I am opposed to all superstition: Muslim, Christian, Jewish or Buddhist.

---

[1] The English edition was banned in April 1959 and the translation was proscribed shortly after this reply.

'I am reading your book *Why I am Not a Christian*. . . You speak of Christ and doubt his ever having lived and then go on to say you believed he was a great man. . . .'

February 19, 1963

Dear Miss Lowler,

It is a pity you have not read my book more carefully, for you entirely confuse three separate issues. The historical evidence for the existence of Christ the man is flimsy. The views attributed to him are another matter. Such views enable one to assess an individual, hypothetical or existing, who might hold them.

Some of the ethical views which purport to come from him are supportable. The hallucinatory conviction that he possessed divinity was shared by many wandering mystics and lunatics of the day. This is of interest primarily to psychologists.

Yours sincerely
Bertrand Russell

'Today I was lunching with a friend who . . . . mentioned . . . that he possessed several autographed photographs of famous opera singers. I replied that aside from an autographed photograph of Jesus Christ (obtainable from a fundamentalist evangelist who broadcasts from Del Rio, Mexico) the only autographed photograph I would prize would be one of Bertrand Russell. . . .'

October 22, 1958

Dear Mr Todd,

Thank you for your very agreeable letter. . . . I regret that I cannot supply an autograph of Jesus Christ. I hope my own will do to be getting on with, and you will find it at the foot of this letter.

Yours sincerely
Bertrand Russell

'I am grateful for your autobiography. Thank you. I have already thanked God. . . .'

May 6, 1968

Dear Miss Bush,

I am pleased that you liked my autobiography, but troubled that you thanked God for it, because that suggests that He has infringed my copyright.

With good wishes,

Yours sincerely
Bertrand Russell

PEACE AND POLITICS

FOREWORD

'The whole point about H-bombs is that they must not be used in any circumstances.'

At a time when the bomb came to symbolize the atavistic forces poised against mankind, Bertrand Russell proved to be the very antithesis, looming large as a champion of humanity. He held that nuclear danger could only be averted by arousing mass public pressure against it. 'It is not acceptance of war but resistance to it which is imperative if we are to survive', he declared.

By 1960 he had plunged into the campaign for mass resistance, addressed CND demonstrators in Trafalgar Square, and exhorted people to civil disobedience as the most effective method of mobilizing public opinion against nuclear war. The following year, aged eighty-nine, he led a mass sit-down outside the Ministry of Defence in Whitehall. He and his wife were sentenced to two months' imprisonment for their part in this and other protests (reduced to one week for reasons of health). In 1962, while the world held its breath during the Cuban crisis, Russell was mediating between Khrushchev and Kennedy. 'The solution to the crisis made the week one of the most worthwhile of my entire life', he stated. Later he was to play a similar role between Nehru and Chou En-lai over the Sino-Indian border dispute. He became increasingly involved in the problems faced by the 'third world', and by 1963 was devoting his energies to the cause for peace in Vietnam.

It was this period, the tension and alarm of the early 'sixties, the hectic days of demonstration and popular reaction against the nuclear peril and threat of war, that earned for Russell the world-wide following and acclaim of millions of ordinary people. As Herbert Gottschalk indicates so aptly in his short biography of Russell:

'Perhaps one day the world will be less interested in Bertrand Russell's philosophical works and in the details of his personal life, than in the splendid example of courage and human dignity he has given us.'

Russell's detractors have sought to revile his unyielding commitment to humanity as though he were trespassing in politics. Popular resistance is a term dreaded in certain quarters, but how much more unpardonable when a real live lord, and philosopher to boot, becomes its chief advocate and begins knocking down all those prestigious pillars he is meant to uphold. The view of these particular critics is both false and absurd. If one takes the trouble to study Russell's life it becomes obvious at once that there is nothing incongruous in his stand against the bomb or the war in Vietnam. On the contrary, his so-called 'political irruptions' evolve from, and are the logical outcome of, his prime concern that all humanity should have a future; thus his support for the victims of apartheid tyranny in southern Africa and for that matter his disapproval of the Afghan war waged by Britain in 1878, which he terms 'my earliest political recollection'.

His latter-day campaigns, although contested on a far wider stage, had their parallel years earlier when he vigorously agitated in favour of peace and conscientious objection against the fraudulence and horror of World War I. It is as well to recall the fierce denunciations and persecution suffered by Russell then. He was fined £100 as author of a 'seditious' anti-war leaflet, abruptly dismissed from his lectureship at Cambridge's Trinity College, banned from the coast for fear that he might signal to enemy submarines, and finally gaoled for six months in 1918. Yet in due course, in cooler light, Russell's views which had shocked so many were accepted as sane, right-minded and even respectable.

Those who concede Bertrand Russell's early achievements, and yet inexplicably denounce his more recent commitments, might well reflect on the consistency with which he championed the cause of human survival. As with past controversies these critics must in time grow to respect the validity of his later strivings. Unless of course a nuclear holocaust interrupts this process and Bertrand Russell's life work comes to naught.

'. . . I have recently read a quotation attributed to you stating that you would gladly crawl on your belly to Moscow to surrender, rather than have your beloved England subjected to a hydrogen bomb attack. I am not surprised to hear this coming from you after all your years of making like an intellectual idiot. . . .

'It is such a pity that your great Country, historically known for its great patriots and men of courage, could produce you, with all the implications of your fear psychology "peace at any price" and in the end, total surrender. Try borrowing a little "guts" from some of your patriotic countrymen. . . .'

September 6, 1960

Sir,

Your letter consists of vulgar abuse. The remark about crawling upon my belly to Moscow is an invention of my opponents, if it has ever been made at all. Nonetheless, if I thought that such a feat were within my powers at the age of eighty-eight and would have any effect towards preserving my compatriots, or any human beings, from the imminent destruction by means of nuclear warfare, I should endeavour to do it, though I fear that I should also have to crawl to Washington. That the extinction of the human race is all too likely to come about in the near future seems to me to be owing largely to the angrily closed minds of rigid dogmatists.

Yours faithfully
Bertrand Russell

———

A reply to a young American student seeking information about Russell's anti-nuclear war activities.

November 27, 1959

Dear Mr Heineman,

. . . I note that among the books you mention *Portraits from Memory* is not included. No doubt the title led you to think that it was not concerned with nuclear war, but the last two items in the book are concerned with the danger of war and the means of preventing it, and there are a number of passages earlier in the book that seem relevant. Another book that you do not mention is *The Vital Letters of Russell, Khrushchev, Dulles*. I send you a copy of this.

You may be interested in some facts and dates as regards my activities. The Bikini Test and the Russian development of H-bombs showed that the peril of nuclear warfare and the ruin that it would cause were both much greater than they had seemed. I emphasized this in a BBC broadcast made on December 23, 1954, which is reprinted in *Portraits from Memory* under the title 'Man's Peril'. The response to this was so astonishingly widespread and favourable that, very shortly after this, I wrote to Einstein suggesting a declaration by a few very eminent men of science, both Communist and Western, on the lines of my broadcast. He emphatically agreed, but said that owing to ill health he must leave most of the work to me. I drew up a draft of the document and sent it to him. Einstein agreed to my draft but the letter announcing his agreement reached me after his death. I secured the signatures of ten very eminent scientists of varying shades of Communist and Western political opinion to the draft which Einstein had approved. I think this was the first time that Communists and anti-Communists had co-operated in such a document. I publicized the document at a press conference on July 9, 1955, attended by the representatives in London of all the leading newspapers of the world including of course the British papers. This conference was televised and broadcast throughout the world. Out of this arose what is called The Pugwash Movement, a series of conferences at which scientists of East and West meet from time to time to discuss dangers and preventives, and to draw up resolutions avoiding bias towards either side. The Movement derives its name from the fact that its first conference took place at Pugwash, Nova Scotia, and was rendered possible by the hospitality and financial support of Mr. Cyrus Eaton who has continued ever since to give his assistance to the Movement. The repeated experience of these Conferences has shown that friendly co-operation between Eastern and Western scientists is entirely possible and that important agreements can be reached. The results of these conferences are published in reports which can be obtained from Professor Eugene Rabinovitch, Editor of the *Bulletin of the Atomic Scientists.*

Since these first happenings, campaigns have been organized in America, Britain and Germany and Japan on the perils of nuclear warfare and the means of avoiding it.

Ever since my Christmas broadcast in 1954, most of my time has been occupied with the question of nuclear warfare. I have received requests for expressions of opinion from very many countries of the West and the East, both Communist and anti-Communist. I am sending you a very small selection of my replies under separate cover.

Yours sincerely
Bertrand Russell

'. . . I believe, as sincerely as you believe the opposite, that a national policy of unilateral nuclear disarmament would increase the probability of our civilization being wiped out. I base my belief on the evidence of history:—

Herod massacring babies.

That humane man Cromwell slaughtering the garrison of Drogheda in 1651.

Stalin killing defenceless kulaks, who incidentally had no American bases on their soil.

Khrushchev sending the tanks in to kill civilians in Hungary who were insufficiently armed and who had no American bases on their soil.

All right then, Suez too, though I am a Tory.

Hitler liquidating 6,000,000 jews who were unarmed, unresisting, and who had no American bases, etc.

I also see:—

Hitler not massacring British prisoners-of-war because we could have retaliated.

Stalin not absorbing West Berlin because of American, British, and French guarantees.

England not invading Scotland after getting a bloody nose at Bannockburn.

And most devastating of all these arguments and one on which all unilateralists must surely stumble, that balanced deterrent,

that equal balance of two powers that melted away unused,—
the poison gas of the last war.

. . . Lord Russell, in all sincerity and some humility, I believe that
if you are right in thinking that we shall all be dead in a year, it
will be because such as you have brought the bombs on our heads
by your unilateral nuclear disarmament. . . .'

June 27, 1962

Dear Mr Young,

Your letter of June 22, which I received this morning, unlike
most of the hostile letters that I receive, is argumentative and not
merely abusive and I am therefore answering it. You begin with a
number of examples of human wickedness. I fully admit that they
illustrate human nature, as to which I have no illusions. But they
do not bear upon the argument of British unilateralism, as I shall
shortly argue, since Britain has no deterrent and America will not
use hers in our defence. I am also not prepared to dispute what
you say about Hitler, Stalin, and Cromwell, and Bannockburn.
As for what you say about gas in the Second War, there were two
reasons for its non-employment: first, the First War had proved
that it is not a decisive weapon; second, everybody had gas
masks.

The positive arguments for British unilateralism are as follows:
Britain has no defence against H-bombs, which could wipe out
the whole population in half an hour. Herman Kahn . . . has
argued very convincingly that, if the Russians wiped out Britain
without attacking the United States, the U.S. would not retaliate
by making war on Russia (see *Survival*, vol. II, No. 2). Both
Khrushchev and Malinovsky, at the time of the U-2 incident and
later, threatened to 'obliterate' any ally of the U.S. which allowed
its territory to be used in a manner which the U.S.S.R. considered
unfriendly. In these circumstances, there is no policy which will
give Britain complete security, except general and universal
nuclear disarmament. Pending such a measure, Britain has to be
content with expedients. In view of Kahn's argument and the
Russian threats, the U.S.S.R. will have less motive for attacking
us if we are neutral than if we remain in NATO. The U.S.S.R.
has not, so far, attacked any neutral. What you, and those who

think as you do, fail to realize is that Britain has no defence whatever against an attack from the U.S.S.R. except to adopt a policy which will make the U.S.S.R. consider such an attack pointless.

There is a further argument for British neutrality: if Russia and America persist in present policies, a nuclear war, sooner or later, is almost certain to occur. The best hope of more conciliatory relations between the two giants is that neutrals will suggest compromise solutions which both sides could adopt without loss of face. This would become much more feasible if Britain were a neutral than it is at present.

I gather that you, in common with most advocates of a British deterrent, have not noticed that in the opinion of the American Government, as expressed recently by McNamara and Dean Rusk, the British deterrent adds nothing to the strength of NATO and the American Government would be glad to see it abandoned. This view had already been expressed by Herman Kahn who considers that Britain is only an emotional liability to the U.S. This American opinion hurts British pride, and is therefore rejected without investigation by those Britons whose patriotism is compatible with the prospect of the complete extermination of our population.

One last point: I did not say that Britons would all be dead within a year. I said only that this was possible and that, if present policies continue, our extermination sooner or later was nearly certain.

Yours sincerely
Bertrand Russell

'. . . I wondered if it might not have reached your ears; the preposterous propaganda being spread from "top-secret" that in the newest nuclear bomb there is no fall-out and no "spread" of danger. . . .'

September 8, 1961

Dear Mrs Bartholomew,
. . . I have heard all the statements pretending that from the newest nuclear bomb there is no fall-out. All these statements are deliberate lies. I had a broadcast discussion on this point with . . .

one of the chief governmental nuclear authorities in the U.S., who boasted that he had discovered how to make 'clean' bombs and that his research towards this end had been dictated by humanitarian motives. I said, 'Then I suppose you have told the Russians about it?' He replied with horror, 'No, that would be illegal!' Was I to conclude that it was only Russian lives that he wished to spare, not American?

Yours sincerely
Bertrand Russell

'. . . Is there any way for people who wish to be among the survivors of the next war, to get together to form a group before that catastrophe happens? Is there a place in the world that might be comparatively safe for them to go. . . .'

December 19, 1958

Dear Mrs Davidson,
. . . I do not think there is much point in trying to find a safe refuge from radio-active poison. I think it is much more useful, both publicly and personally, to join those who are engaged in trying to prevent a nuclear war. . . .

If, however, you wish to find a comparatively safe region, I think one may say that the Southern hemisphere is safer than the Northern and that it grows progressively safer as you approach the South Pole.

Yours sincerely
Bertrand Russell

'. . . Thanks for your letter. When I first read it my husband and I received the impression that you were pulling our legs when you said, "The Southern Hemisphere is safer than the Northern and it grows progressively safer as you approach the South Pole". But now, some weeks later I am not so sure, since I have heard of quite a few families here who have gone to New Zealand. *Were* you spoofing us, or do you think there *is* some value in our idea of trying to avoid radio active fallout if possible? . . .'

February 23, 1959

Dear Mrs Davidson,

. . . I was not pulling your leg in recommending the Southern Hemisphere on the assumption that there were a war between Russia and the West. If there were a war between China and Australia, the Southern Hemisphere would of course be very dangerous.

Yours sincerely
Bertrand Russell

'[I suggest this slogan] . . . "Disarm—or Pay Shelters for All Peoples!" . . . since those who are ready to destroy the majority of the human race, are ready to survive *their own war*: According to the documentation I have the USA and the USSR have enough shelters to come out of a nuclear world war as *victors,* with about *one hundred million survivals* each! While the great majority of the rest of the human race, having no shelters and too poor to pay for them, would be wiped out— It is quite understandable why the rulers of Russia and the United States are making threats of war and expressing their "courage"— They are owners of the best shelters!'

December, 1962

Dear Mr Fekete,

. . . I cannot agree that shelters should be made for everyone. We shall not gain protection from multi-megaton thermo-nuclear weapons by building shelters; even the 'experts' employed by governments are beginning to admit that. Modern weapons demand shelters of a quite new order, and their cost is prohibitive. It is doubtful, moreover, whether many people would be able to reach them at the short notice to be expected.

Perhaps the most important argument against shelters is that they help to foster the illusion of defence and safety against hydrogen bombs. In this way docile populations are created which are

71

more ready to accept the possibility of war. It is not acceptance of war but resistance to it which is imperative if we are to survive.

Yours sincerely
Bertrand Russell

'. . . There is an immense amount of money tied up in "defence" contracts in the States. The larger firms hire retired army men to lobby for them, and run very powerful lobbies in the U.S. senate, and put out very efficient propaganda. This is going to be a very formidable obstacle to disarmament. . . . A great many people are concerned about the world situation, but the ordinary man is filled with a sense of futility when he considers his capacity to alter the state of affairs. . . .'

May 13, 1962

Dear Sir,

Your letter to me is a most fascinating one, but I should point out to you that I have taken great pains to show the connection between the expenditure on defence and the role of defence in the United States. I have decried the military-industrial complex and in several recent articles have concentrated on this difficulty.

I am enclosing for your interest some recent literature of mine including an article for the *Bulletin of Atomic Scientists* in which I outlined the danger from America's Pentagon and the business men who are in league with it.

As for your suggestion that men feel a sense of futility, that is part of the argument I have been making in this country since 1945. You are quite right, it is not apathy, but a great sense of helplessness which cripples people. The Committee of 100 is a movement of mass resistance the purpose of which is to make available to people a method of protest consonant with the overwhelming danger. . . .

Thank you very much for writing.

Yours sincerely
Bertrand Russell

'. . . the prosperity of Britain and America is based very largely on the armaments industry. If our Government were to agree to a really substantial degree of disarmament they would cause unemployment on a vast scale. . . . It does seem to me that the heads of the Communist countries have come to the conclusion that there is not going to be a nuclear war. Having decided that, all their subsequent actions tie up. The call for disarmament by Mr. K. is *genuine*. If there is going to be no war, armaments are a shocking waste of money. . . . So I am brought to two conclusions. 1. The Russians *mean what they say* when they call for disarmament. 2. The West do not and cannot disarm without endangering the whole structure of their society. . . .'

January 2, 1961

Dear Mr Davie,

. . . I agree with you in what you say about Khrushchev's desire to avoid a war, but I think he is impulsive and things like the U-2 incident may make him lose his balance. As regards the economic consequences of disarmament, I find that Big Business in America does not take the gloomy view that is often taken and to which you incline. *Nation's Business,* the organ of the U.S. Chamber of Commerce, published an article in October 1959, called 'What Peace would do to You'. This article was surprisingly optimistic, but gave what seemed to be good reasons for its views. Another article appeared in *Think* in January, 1960, by Senator Hubert H. Humphrey, called 'After Disarmament What?' This took the same optimistic view. I think one must conclude that the leaders of Big Business in America do not consider the present level of armaments production essential to American prosperity. I hope they are right. In any case, on this point their voice is authoritative. They argue that conversion of plant to peace-time uses will not be very difficult.

Yours sincerely
Bertrand Russell

'. . . I am taking the liberty of sending you under separate cover a copy of the manuscript *Inspection for Disarmament—A Study in*

Technical Feasibility. This project has just been completed . . . and we are most eager to get critical comment on the manuscript. . . .'

March 8, 1958

Dear Professor Melman,

Thank you for your letter and for the manuscript which has just reached me. I am glad that the work has been done, but I do not feel capable of 'critical comment'. It seems to me that you need three experts: a detective, a security officer, and a manager of an explosives factory. It is not the kind of matter about which I can form an opinion.

Yours sincerely
Bertrand Russell

———

'*Suggest great powers flip a coin.*
1. Leaders may need an "out" from their dilemma.
2. Those recommending a toss are in a better position than those favouring the idea, "better red than dead". . . .
3. Religious influence—greater on the Western team—[who] may believe they have a mystical advantage in the contest. That is; would the infinite being leave the odds at 50–50? After the toss, how could they complain? . . .'

March 9, 1962

Dear Mr McGregor,

Thank you for your recent letter, suggesting that the problems between the two blocs should be solved by a series of tosses of a coin. The present method of solving disputes, by threatening to murder hundreds of millions of people, is so lunatic that it would seem that any alternative would be an improvement. However, it seems to me that it is by rational argument alone that we can hope to keep the human species in existence.

I am most interested by your idea that the West would expect to gain some mystical advantage from the power of God on its side. I should hesitate however to recommend a procedure which would have a fifty per cent chance of seeming to prove the existence of a deity.

> *Yours sincerely*
> *Bertrand Russell*

'. . . I have followed with interest and no small measure of devotion your activities in the cause of the salvation of mankind from himself. . . . When so much is at stake as at present it appears, probably the only way in which public consciousness could be aroused would be the simultaneous fasting of prominent men . . . until the total and immediate abandonment of nuclear testing a nd armament. . . .'

February 1, 1962

Dear Mr Best,

. . . Your suggestion that I should take part in a simultaneous fast with prominent men from all over the world, demanding an end to nuclear testing, I am afraid I do not think is likely to achieve success. The power-elites of the United States, Britain, France, and the Soviet Union have never shown themselves particularly concerned at the fate of those of us who reject the political tenets that the great powers all hold in common. I do not feel that any solution to our problems can come from the action of a few men whom the world likes to call prominent. It is the great mass of people all over the planet, who do not wish to be sacrificed on the altar of national prestige, that will alone be able to force the criminal lunatics of the Pentagon and the Kremlin to their senses. The apathy that we see all around us stems from no lack of concern, but from a deep sense of powerlessness. We have found in Britain that when we offer a means of struggle both compatible with the peril we are fighting, and available to ordinary people in their tens of thousands, the popular apathy is replaced by a determination to undergo any sacrifice, from imprisonment to alienation from friends and family, that will help in the prevention of a nuclear war. There are no short cuts: we have to build an international movement of mass resistance to nuclear annihilation. I

75

do not know whether we shall succeed, but I am convinced that we must make the attempt. . . .

Yours sincerely
Bertrand Russell

———————

This letter suggests Russell use the gramophone record to 'publicize' the horrors of atomic warfare, as follows:

'. . . If one talks brutally about the terrors of atomic warfare, people tend not to listen, but if one were to talk about these horrors and terrors, describing, for example, in biting wit, how people would probably react towards one another in situations of extreme stress, the message would probably hit home and make for the sort of thing where anybody who had bought the record would insist on playing it for his friends. For example: "you know that when you, at gunpoint, turn your next door neighbour away from the questionable safety of your atom bomb shelter you will certainly *finish* any friendship with him and, what is more, you may, by so doing, *finish him*! . . ." '

March 25, 1962

Dear Sir,
. . . I do not like the suggestion of a record of bad jokes concerning the consequences of nuclear war. I am not interested in marketing detergents or even in reforming the Salvation Army. The issues are vast in perspective and require more respect for the intelligence of those to whom one is speaking. I am asking people to act in the name of conscience and not to laugh in the cause of evasion.

Yours sincerely
Bertrand Russell

. . . It may be that due to the fact that we did not clearly explain our idea, there was some misunderstanding as to the intent. . . . I don't suggest that we make a record of 'bad jokes' concerning the consequences of nuclear warfare. I do, however, suggest that the remarks be deadly cynical in their nature and I do think also, that one unexplored area of promotion and publicity is the phonograph record. . . .

April 16, 1962

Dear Sir,
. . . I am afraid that I understood perfectly well your proposal in your earlier letter, and I am not disposed to make a recording such as you suggest. I suggest that you take recordings of MacMillan and Kennedy: their cynicism is something I am glad I cannot excel.

Yours sincerely
Bertrand Russell

The following was Russell's reply to one of the many letters he received supporting his intervention in the Cuban 'Missiles' crisis.

November 19, 1962

Dear Mr. Casselberry,
Thank you for your kind wishes. I was pleased to receive them.
As you might appreciate, the crisis was such that it was not clear that we should survive the week, but I can assure you that the solution to the crisis made the week one of the most worthwhile of my entire life.
With good wishes,

Yours sincerely
Bertrand Russell

'. . . Recently you hailed Mr. Khrushchev as a man of peace for deciding to withdraw gracefully from the Cuban crisis. . . . was [it not] due to fear of the superior might of the U.S., and not out of any real love for peace? . . .'

77

December 6, 1962

Dear Mr Anjan,

. . Mr. Khrushchev took unilateral action to ease the Cuban crisis because he had a greater sense of responsibility than President Kennedy. The great powers were set on a collision course, and if Mr. Khrushchev had shown the same firmness as President Kennedy, we should not be alive today.

> *Yours sincerely*
> *Bertrand Russell*

'. . . I would be interested in knowing why you came out against the United States of America in its stand in the Cuban blockade instead of criticizing the Soviet Union for sending those goods to Cuba while all the time guaranteeing that they would never take such action. I am presently studying your philosophy in college now and can see no basis for this action on your part. . . .'

December 14, 1962

Dear Mr Campbell,

. . . I criticised the United States because it threatened to sink Soviet ships on the high seas, knowing full well that such action would initiate general nuclear warfare.

The United States has no more right to determine the armoury in Cuba than the Soviet Union has in Turkey, Italy, Britain, or in any of the many other countries harbouring American bases around the Communist perimeter.

> *Yours sincerely*
> *Bertrand Russell*

'. . . a large majority of us Americans agreed with President Kennedy in the steps he took to remove the missile bases from Cuba, steps which you termed "contemptible". The attempt to establish those bases was of course just one more step toward the incineration of mankind. . . .

'Can you not use the great respect which you command throughout the world to try to improve communication among the people of various nations either by the exchange of newspapers or by some other means? . . .'

January 24, 1963

Dear Mr Ceccarelli,

. . . I have never opposed the removal of nuclear installations in Cuba and am glad that this was, in fact, carried out. It was not the desire for their removal that I thought contemptible, but the fact that the matter was not negotiated. Also I object to it being said that Cuba has no right to go Communist if it wishes.

Your suggestion that newspapers might be exchanged by countries involved in the Cold War might, if implemented, make a small contribution to easing tension, however, the fact that most Western newspapers are owned by wealthy men who have no desire to see the Cold War terminated would create difficulties for even this modest proposal.

Yours sincerely
Bertrand Russell

'. . . I understand you were displeased with America's action recently in the Cuban Crisis. Is this correct? Do you feel it would have been better if the Communists had been allowed to establish their missiles there? . . . If you had a neighbour who continually came to your house and took something of yours, well what would you do? You might allow them to have something . . . but what if they wanted something more? Is it very intelligent to give everything away?'

January 12, 1963

Dear Mr Gass,

. . . Your analogy about a neighbour who continually comes to one's house and takes something is quite misleading. If I had such a neighbour, I should certainly not destroy him and everybody

79

else who lived in the same street. That, however, is the threatened response of your own President to a crisis situation.

It is, moreover, absurd to suggest that the Communists have stolen anything in Cuba. The Cuban Government has just as much, or little, right to build bases in Cuba as has the American Government in Turkey, Japan, Italy, Britain, or anywhere else on the Communist periphery.

Yours sincerely
Bertrand Russell

———

'I'm writing to you to ask if you could tell me how I should address a letter to Mr. Khrushchev. You see I feel I must write and thank him, on behalf of all the ordinary people such as myself, for his decision in the recent Cuban Crisis. . . . and wondered if you have an organisation which one may join. . . .'

December 7, 1962

Dear Miss Graves,

Thank you for your letter of November 29th. The address you request is: Mr. N. Khrushchev, Chairman of the Council of Ministers, Moscow, U.S.S.R.

If you write to the Secretary of the Committee of 100, 13 Goodwin Street, London, you will be put in touch with the local Committee of 100.

I was heartened to learn of your support for our cause.

Yours sincerely
Bertrand Russell

———

'. . . it appeared to my great surprise that you considered the Chinese case very much stronger than you had thought of and that you were also in doubt who the aggressor was. You also attributed the withdrawal of the Chinese forces to the peaceful intentions of Chou En Lai's Government. . . . It is not difficult to find out now who the aggressor was. How cunning, how aggressive and deceitful the Chinese have been is now an open secret.

They have even refused to accept the advice of neutral and disinterested nations. They have not agreed to the simple proposals made by six neutral nations in the Colombo conference. . . . China's real intentions are clear. . . . She wants to be master of Asia and thus destroy the world's peace. . . . It is not clear what made the Chinese Government order a cease-fire. We all think it is a trick. The Chinese are notoriously famous in preparing tricks and staging them as real facts. . . .'

April 24, 1963

Dear Mr Chadha,
 . . . The problem of the Sino-Indian border conflict is unfortunately not so simple as you imply. The Chinese have accepted all but two of the Colombo proposals, and their reasons for rejecting these two appear to me to be entirely valid. The Indian refusal to commence any negotiations until the Chinese have accepted the Colombo proposals in toto is not helpful. I am in touch with both Governments, however, and am still hopeful that negotiations may start before disaster overtakes both parties.

As a lifelong friend of India, I am distressed at the mood of belligerence which has overtaken your country. Your own letter, in attributing every conceivable wickedness to the Chinese, is an admirable example of this.

Yours sincerely
Bertrand Russell

'. . . Unfortunately in all these wars against the British my family was involved. These blunders were quite unnecessary of course but I imagine they were largely due to the fault of a few politicians who didn't understand the mind of the Afghans . . . the relations between the British and the Afghans during these years have been very unfortunate. . . .'

June 9, 1963

Dear Aslam Effendi,
 . . . I am much interested by what you have to say about the past relations between the British and the Afghans. The Afghan War

of 1878, of which my family strongly disapproved, is my earliest political recollection. . . .

    With all good wishes,

> *Yours sincerely*
> *Bertrand Russell*

'. . . Haile Selassie's name added to that of your sponsors [of the Bertrand Russell Peace Foundation] gives me thought. Rightly or wrongly I have had him grouped with other U.S.-British henchmen round the world. At the time of the last war I gathered there was no need to shed tears at Mussolini turning him out. His reinstatement was back to the old bad order. . . .'

> September 14, 1964

Dear Mr Beasley,

. . . As you know, I consider the most urgent issue facing us to be the avoidance of nuclear war and all my energies are directed to removing the danger of world war and eliminating the Cold War with its attendant injustices.

    Haile Selassie is a feudal ruler and an autocrat, but he has performed a very valuable service in settling the Algerian-Moroccan Border dispute and in assisting neutralism in Africa through his efforts on behalf of African Unity which has its headquarters in Addis Ababa.

    Mr. Nehru, who was my friend, pursued policies opposed to the Cold War, although he was not successful in seriously changing the pattern of poverty in India.

    . . . I hope you will see, therefore, that the support of all who wish to help to work for peace is welcome by us, for the question of peace and war transcends all of us. . . .

> *Yours sincerely*
> *Bertrand Russell*

'. . . My mother tongue is Arabic, but I was fortunate enough to have a chance to study English . . . I was able to read some of your work. I was impressed with your clarity and the high degree of honesty . . . I wished to hear your frank opinion about the Suez war and the Palestine issue and the Algerian war. . . .'

June 15, 1960

Dear Mr Mohammed Radwan Hamwi,
  Thank you for your letter of June 3. Here are my answers:
  1. I thought the Suez War a blunder and a crime, and said so publicly at the time.
  2. I think it was a mistake to establish a Jewish State in Palestine, but it would be a still greater mistake to try to get rid of it now that it exists. I strongly disapprove of the mutual intolerance displayed by Jews and Arabs.
  3. I think Algeria should be independent under a treaty giving some assurance for the safety of long-term French residents.

Yours very truly
Bertrand Russell

A reply to a letter seeking support for imprisoned leaders of the Negro people of Harlem.

March 31, 1965

Dear Mr McAdoo,
  . . . I wholeheartedly condemn the shocking persecution in New York of those who speak up on behalf of the oppressed Negroes of Harlem.
  . . . Harlem is a city occupied by an oppressive army serving what amounts to an outside power. In Harlem there are more rats than people and more cockroaches than rats. Its inhabitants are brutalised at every moment of their lives by police, poverty and indignity. If in any country in the world city after city rose up for days on end, taking to the streets, battling with the police, barricading boulevards and smashing shops, it would rightly be called a rebellion or revolution. In the United States it is called a black riot.
  Nothing more clearly indicates the hand of oppression in America than the indictment of American radicals for having instigated these riots. Mr. Epton has been indicted for trying to

overthrow the Government of the State of New York. Five others face long gaol terms. The Grand Jury which has returned these indictments holds those radicals who have championed the Negro cause responsible for the black revolution. How pathetic. The very people responsible for the decades of misery in Harlem indict the passionate opponents of their practice.

This is a struggle which will not end until the system of society which allows these conditions to obtain and such Grand Juries to wield power is overthrown. Were I in New York I should certainly be guilty of trying to overthrow the Government of the State of New York. Anything less is an evasion of responsibility in the face of brutality and injustice. . . .

With all good wishes,

Yours sincerely
Bertrand Russell

'. . . I am an American Negro involved in research work . . . my particular project concerns the touchy problem of one of America's favorite pastimes of days gone by—lynching. Now almost extinct, it once flourished mostly in the southern regions of the United States. I would be forever grateful for your comments in a letter on this particular subject. . . .'

April 30, 1964

Dear Mr Glover

Thank you very much for your letter. There is a great need for serious study of lynching in the American South which is by no means extinct according to information which I receive from time to time. The behaviour of Southern American police appears to be such that wanton murder can be indulged in without fear of reprisal. I think that it is most important to document the true nature of brutality in the American south and the full extent of it.

With good wishes,

Yours sincerely
Bertrand Russell

A reply to a despairing opponent of American intervention in Vietnam.

November 26, 1965

Dear Mr Robertson,

... I much sympathise with your feelings of disheartenment, but it is inevitable that effective opposition to the cruel war of aggression waged by the United States will elicit crude hostility from those who promote it.

I should not despair of the people of the United States, however, for the American people are not allowed to know the true character of the war waged by their government. It is the duty of those of us who understand the injustice and cruelty involved to educate and inform our fellow citizens.

The war in Vietnam is not the first, and will not be the last such war waged by American imperialism. It may be hoped that as the peoples of the world struggle for their emancipation, the people of the United States will come to understand more clearly the nature of their government, and in time overcome it.

I am sending you recent literature concerning our work, and wish you all success in your efforts to resist injustice, for which we have great admiration.

Yours sincerely
Bertrand Russell

Russell replies to questions on the Cold War and anti-communism in Britain and America.

April 26, 1963

Dear Professor Gould,

Thank you for your recent letter. I shall try to answer your questions briefly.

1. Members of the British Communist Party have not been entirely free from prosecution. The treatment they have received, however, has been much better than that accorded to their colleagues in many other countries because few people in this country suppose that the British Communist Party is a threat to the

nation. If Communists here had been imprisoned more frequently, there is little doubt that this treatment would also have been given to other groups holding dissident political opinions. It is impossible to create machinery for the suppression of one viewpoint without it being used more widely to suppress a whole variety of dissident opinions. In that sense, members of the British Labour Party have had more freedom than if Communists were imprisoned frequently. On the other hand, members of the Labour Party, and in particular Labour Members of Parliament, have shown little anxiety to use their freedom and have, for the most part, endorsed the pursuit of the Cold War and the maintenance of security—the very policies which reduce drastically political freedom.

2. Britain enjoys greater freedom of speech in this area than the United States for a number of reasons. The Cold War is polarised in the Soviet Union and the United States, and one would, therefore, expect to find dissident opinion most carefully controlled or suppressed in these two countries. In the United States this suppression has become so complete that it has created the conditions for widespread fanaticism. Economic interests which ensure American support of dozens of feudal dictatorships around the globe make it necessary to propound a devil-theory about Communism, and this results in an appalling self-righteousness which bears no relationship to the facts and cannot tolerate freedom of speech or independence of mind. The totalitarian pressures of the Cold War make the United States and the Soviet Union more similar in their intolerance, and the degree of freedom of speech in Britain will be very much dictated by the degree of British involvement in the Cold War.

I hope that these replies are of some help to you.

Yours sincerely
Bertrand Russell

'. . . South Africa has outlawed Communism for the sake of survival. . . . Sentences of death for Saboteurs are as right as your execution of various Spies in the post war years. May I ask if you have any personal experience of our country? . . . I have lived in

South Africa for 43 years and have just completed a car trip in Great Britain and not once have been involved in an acrimonious argument about my country. I wear a blazer which tells them where I'm from, too. . . . You have only 8% non-white here and growing steadily, but I hear rumblings. I wish you could talk to some of the hundreds of Kenya farmers who are pouring into South Africa and hear what they have to say. . . .'

September 20, 1963

Dear Mr Dexter,

Your letter in no way impresses me. I do not sanction ruthless cruelty because of the political views of the victims. South Africa is a tyranny over the majority of its inhabitants and rules by brute force.

Yours faithfully
Bertrand Russell

Russell replies to a correspondent who is opposed to the Apartheid regime in South Africa and who asks for guidance for a local Anti-Apartheid Committee.

November 27, 1964

Dear Mr Hougham,

Thank you very much for your letter which I read with care. I think it probable that non-violent action will not succeed in altering the regime in South Africa. As with most industrial totalitarian countries, organised revolution is extremely difficult and non-violent resistance even more so. The regime in South Africa makes open opposition impossible and, therefore, minimises the opportunities of organised non-violent opposition. Having said this, however, I should point out that it is very difficult to stop violence once it begins. The Algerian revolution cost one and a half million lives out of a population of 8 million. Comparable disaster in Britain would involve the lives of 6 million people and a devastation of the entire country. The end result is a government dependent upon its army and it is because victorious revolutions invariably succeed through the discipline

87

of a determined guerilla army that they soon enter a Bonapartist phase. To answer your queries specifically:

1. It is presumptuous for those of us not faced with conditions such as those which obtain in South Africa to determine the form of struggle. I believe our efforts in Britain should be concentrated on making known the nature of the regime and on mobilising public opinion so that the British Government can be induced to apply pressure. I do not believe anti-apartheid organisations should dissociate themselves from nationalist movements advocating violence.

2. In the event of outbreak of violence in South Africa, the campaign for external pressure of an economic order should be stepped up. United Nations intervention is rarely beneficial because the U.N. itself is so much the centre of Cold War power politics. Until this ceases to be true, intrusion of the U.N. will mean little more than the introduction of American power into the area concerned. This was evident in the Congo. If Nationalist movements seek assistance from Cold War powers, it will, without doubt, increase the danger of world war. There is no remedy other than seeking economic sanctions against the offending governments. The longer pressure against the government of South Africa is delayed, the more dangerous and violent the explosion will be. There is no escaping this. Western investments in South Africa are colossal. If the government is tolerated by those who hold these investments until the final explosion of violence, the situation will be even more grave.

In short, the task of those seeking to oppose apartheid is to work for the maximum pressure against the regime from the outside. There is no way to remove the spectre of violence short of that. Violence is endemic where governments of this order hold sway.

Yours sincerely
Bertrand Russell

'. . . The government . . . intends to strengthen the power of the Minister of Education and the presidents of universities over faculties and individual teachers, and to exclude Marxism. Most of our university teachers and students oppose this bill. Before the War . . . we Japanese experienced control over freedom of thought and study at university. . . . Some of us may be exiled by the bill, if it is presented to and passed by Parliament. . . .'

January 16, 1963

Dear Dr Iwamatsu,

. . . I am disgusted to learn of the Government's bill outlawing the teaching and discussion of Marxism in universities and extending political control over faculties and individual teachers.

I consider this a most grave indication of the onset of full-blown authoritarian militarism in Japan and I wish to make my own protest about it. If you care to make this letter publicly known please do not hesitate to do so.

Do inform me of further developments and if there is any reprisal against you, as you indicate, be assured that I shall raise the matter publicly in this country and elsewhere.

With good wishes,

Yours sincerely
Bertrand Russell

'My bookseller, who is commissioned to supply me with everything by you that appears in the German language, recently sent me a copy of *Skepsis* [*Sceptical Essays*]. . . . I was again able to take my usual intense pleasure in the fact that, despite its sharp-minded intelligence and its rational logic, everything is so simply expressed that any reasonably educated layman can understand it with ease. In the middle of my enjoyment, however, I received a slap in the face . . . and I had to re-read several times to see whether I had read right. But there it was in black and white: *"In Switzerland it is not only legally permissible to murder a communist; the assassin can even claim in his defence at his second crime that he is a first offender".'*

December 8, 1965

Dear Mr Willi,

Your letter of December 1st urgently demands an explanation. The facts as I understand them are as follows:

In the early days of the Russian Revolution the Soviet government sent ambassadors to the countries which had been allies of Russia and to some others. These ambassadors were not acknowledged by the nations concerned to have ambassadorial status. I myself was in prison with Litvinov who was sent as Soviet ambassador to Great Britain. The man whom the Russians selected as Soviet ambassador to Switzerland[1] was murdered by a fanatic who, though his guilt was manifest, was not punished. Afterwards, when the assassin committed another crime, he was allowed to plead as a first offender. I no longer have the documents which prove this, but I know that at the time they were convincing. I know also that for some time the Soviet government refused to allow any of its diplomatic representatives to travel in Switzerland.

It is true that later developments made the whole story seem incredible, but I do not think its truth can be questioned. If I have got the facts wrong at any point I will gladly make a public correction.

With thanks for your kind words,

Yours sincerely
Bertrand Russell

'. . . I wrote you some months ago pointing out that the real cause of war is Capitalism, but in your reply you did not agree. I gather you have since recognised the terrible nature of this evil force and that the only way to make war impossible is to eradicate the system which is based on the exploitation of labour for personal gain. When this is eliminated we are left with Socialism or Communism. Thus the sooner we join up with Russia the better for mankind. . . .'

March 26, 1963

Dear Mr Horwood,
. . . I am surprised you should think my antipathy to capitalism a new phenomenon as I have written against it since 1896. My dislike for capitalism is about equal to my distaste for communism,

[1] Vaclav Vorovsky. The assassin was a White Guard emigre.

but neither of these antagonisms on my part remotely compare with my detestation of nuclear warfare. I hope that this makes my position quite clear.

With good wishes,

Yours sincerely
Bertrand Russell

The following is a reply to an appeal seeking Russell's support in a campaign against blood-sports in Britain.

November 26, 1960

Dear Sir,

. . . I am in entire agreement with you about fox-hunting, which I abominate. I very much dislike cruelty to animals, but I am so occupied with anti-nuclear work that I do not feel I can take on anything else. Since a nuclear war would probably kill all animals, I feel that what I am doing is also fighting their cause. . . .

Yours sincerely
Bertrand Russell

'. . . I should be very grateful if you could give me a statement of your views on the question of conscientious objection to modern war, and on pacifism. . . .'

April 30, 1960

Dear Mr Freeman,

. . . As for my own view on conscientious objection, I have never been opposed to *all* war. I thought and still think that the Second World War was justified, but the First was not. I should have been a conscientious objector in the First World War if I had not been above military age. I do not think that in the nuclear age conscientious objection can play a very important part unless it conquers the people who have to press the button which will cause us all to die. I do not accept complete pacifism as a creed, and I think that each war must be judged on its merits. I think that if a World Government were established, it would be justified in using force against rebels. But in the present state of the world, I do not see how any war can do anything except harm.

Yours sincerely
Bertrand Russell

'. . . Permit me respectfully to offer a comment on *Portraits from Memory*. You deplore the Entente Cordiale of 1904 and hold that Britain should have stood aside from the conflict in 1914. Germany would then have defeated France, Italy and Russia. Militarism flushed with victory, would then have been triumphant and I cannot believe that such liberal forces as there may have been would have had any hope against it. . . .'

February 20, 1957

Dear Mr Blyth,
. . . I entirely agree with you that the consequences of a German victory in the First War would have been deplorable. My argument is that they would have been less deplorable than the consequences of our victory. We said it was a war against militarism, but militarism has steadily increased since 1918. We said it was a war for democracy, but democracy has steadily diminished. We said it was a war to end war, and it was followed by an even worse war. Both the Nazis and the Communists resulted from the ferocity of the First War. In all likelihood, neither would have achieved power if the First War had been brief. I repeat, I am not suggesting that the world would have been pleasant if the Germans had won quickly; but are you suggesting that the world *is* pleasant?

Yours sincerely
Bertrand Russell

'. . . In order for world government to be brought about, you say in your essay "The Future of Mankind" that force will be required. I agree. You also say that a world government brought about through the actions of the United States is much more to be desired than that which would result from Soviet control. Again,

I agree. But I disagree with your point that any world government, even that brought about by the Soviets, is to be desired. . . .'

December 7, 1962

Dear Mr Carpenter,

I apologise for the delay in replying to your letter of October 23, which I was pleased to receive.

The questions which you raise concerning world government are as difficult as they are important. I still believe that any world government—even one brought about by the Soviets—is preferable to no world government. Soviet domination should strenuously be avoided, but world thermo-nuclear war even more so. Militarism and lust for power may be temporary; the ending of human life on the planet would be permanent.

I am not convinced, of course, that these are the only alternatives open to us. Nor can I forget that the Western world, in seeking to counter Communism, has already in fact abandoned many of the values which supposedly distinguish it.

Perhaps you would be interested to read my recent book *Has Man A Future?*

Yours sincerely
Bertrand Russell

. . . I am a member of the C.N.D. to which my parents are violently opposed. They have sent me this cutting from the *Telegraph* of some weeks ago [quoting your earlier opinions] in an endeavour to allege your infidelity to the cause of peace. . . .

' "I think there are only two possibilities—co-existence and co-extinction. If you're not going to find a way of co-existing, the human race will cease to exist. And I think we've got to co-exist. I think the Russians have got to realise that, and we have got to realise it.

' "I am perfectly aware that we shan't get the Russians to realise it unless we have very powerful armaments. We must have sufficiently powerful armaments to make the Russians think a war is not worth while. That, I think is obvious. I am not at all inclined to urge disarmament at the present time—not at all." '

93

December 21, 1961

Dear Mrs. Wilson,

. . . The cutting you enclose is not unusual. Let me first of all say that it is in no way an accurate statement of any opinion I have held. It is a very favourite practice of newspapers and of intellectually bankrupt politicians to distort earlier statements of mine. Nonetheless it must be stated that my views have changed during the past two decades and for the simple reason that events and circumstances have changed as well. I have felt it essential to avoid a world war. I have advocated those things which have seemed to me to be most likely to achieve peace. I supported, for example, the Baruch plan designed to internationalise atomic power because I believed that without some such scheme a disastrous arms race was inevitable. At the time I urged the Americans to insist emphatically on the scheme and even to inform Stalin that they would contemplate war if agreement on atomic energy could not be had. I emphasise that I did not advocate a war but urged the Americans to convey the intensity of their feeling that the internationalisation of atomic power was essential to survival.

It is important to make clear that I also attacked the American refusal to give assurance that the United Nations would not be a mere Western instrument so as to allay the fears of Stalin that such internationalisation would be merely a trick to keep nuclear power exclusively in Western hands.

Because I have advocated different ways of securing peace in the past the charge of inconsistency is often levelled. I do not mind this for the failure to adapt one's thought to the exigencies of changing conditions is a certain sign of intellectual stagnation and of dogmatic indifference to fact.

I repeat that the particular passage sent to you is fabricated. I have never stated that I was opposed to disarmament or that co-existence could be furthered by an arms race. Emphatically it is the case that I feel convinced that those who so argue are force-marching mankind to oblivion. Rockets on a hair-trigger, H-bomber non-stop patrols, completely faulty radar, fanatics in control of the Pentagon—these are the sources of our malaise and provide the statistical certainty that men will perish in agony

94

while the pundits and the consistently indifferent lie their way to hell.

Yours sincerely
Bertrand Russell

P.S. Please note the appendices in *Common Sense and Nuclear Warfare*.

'... I am a $15\frac{1}{2}$ years old schoolboy and would be greatly obliged if you would consider my theory of the marches that are organized by your committee. I am very much against the H-Bomb and would like to see it banned. I also think that the way in which your members are going about it is wrong. I think that if your members tried to consider what it is costing this country for the police control and the stupidity ... of squatting on the public highway thus annoying and causing inconvenience to the general public. ... I would be greatly obliged if you would reply to me giving me some reasons why you are marching and squatting on the pavement and roadways. ...'

December 13, 1962

Dear Mr Martin,

Thank you for your recent letter. Football matches, motor car rallies, Royal occasions and many other sporting events cause the police much inconvenience and expense, but nobody suggests that these should be curtailed. Marches and sit-downs are merely concerned with the survival of man on this planet, and, therefore, according to your argument, ought to be stopped. I think you will agree that this is a curious attitude.

Yours sincerely
Bertrand Russell

'... Our President, John F. Kennedy, is coming to Milwaukee for a visit to the local Democratic Party headquarters. We, holding pacific ideals, wish to inform Mr Kennedy by peaceful demonstration of our views on his continuation of nuclear bomb testing. None of our group has any desire to instigate a riot during the President's stay, nor have we any craving to be arrested as the result of our convictions. Therefore, the members of our group, who are from fifteen to eighteen years of age, anxiously await your advice on holding such a demonstration. In view of your activities and concern with youth, we felt it proper to beseech you for guidance in this matter. . . .'

April 19, 1962

Dear Mr Cukurs,

Thank you very much for your interesting letter. I should at once say that I cannot suggest any form of demonstration which one can guarantee will not lead to arrest. However, I would suggest that you consider picketing the entrance to the party headquarters, or the route along which Kennedy will travel, with posters and placards explaining your views. You could also have a leaflet printed at a fairly small cost, and distribute it among the crowd, or throw it into the President's path. It would seem to me that there are three considerations to bear in mind in order that your protest may be as effective as possible. In the first place, the incident that a number of young people are utterly opposed to American atmospheric testing should be firmly imprinted on Kennedy's mind. Secondly, you should ensure by previously contacting the Press that as much publicity for your action is obtained as possible. Thirdly, as many people as are there should clearly see your physical presence, as distortion in the Press will enable many readers to ignore the real nature of your action, whereas it is difficult (or at least *more* difficult) for people to distort what they themselves see.

I am sending you some literature about the Committee of 100 which you may find useful, and some of my recent speeches and articles. Please make any use of these that you are able.

With best wishes,

Yours sincerely
Bertrand Russell

'. . . the forthcoming demonstration at the Air Ministry poses, for me, a great problem, and one which faces thousands in my position. I have taken part in previous demonstrations and have been arrested on two occasions. . . . I have had trouble both at home and with my work as a student and a teacher because of my beliefs, and I find myself now in the position of having to decide either to renounce my work as a teacher by again being arrested and carrying my belief to the practical conclusions of going to prison, or returning to my profession and becoming one of thousands who silently agree, but are of no practical use at all in furthering the vital call for nuclear sanity. . . . I know of many who face the identical problem, yet if the decision involved only ourselves it would be easier. But it involves parents and families, who have both supported through student years, and require support now. I argue that it is for them as much as any that I should participate whole-heartedly in demonstrations. Have I this right? . . .'

Dear Sir,

August 9, 1962

. . . Your problem is one which faces all who contemplate taking part in demonstrations involving civil disobedience. It is a difficult problem and I think the answer in each case must depend upon the particular circumstances of that case. At the same time, for those who believe, as I do, that the total destruction of the population of Britain and of a large part of the population of other countries may occur at any moment and is likely to occur within ten years, it is difficult to put supposed private duty ahead of a public duty which involves protecting one's immediate circle as well as the rest of the world. If all who think as you do protest, the danger may be averted. This is impossible unless protests are very widespread and emphatic. I should not feel inclined to blame those who hang back for the sort of reasons that you indicate, but I could only give positive praise to those who do not hang back. I think it is also worth remembering that, if protests are sufficiently widespread, it will be impossible to victimize any of those concerned except the leaders.

Yours sincerely
Bertrand Russell

'. . . May I have some lines from you on what *The Times* would (or would not) say about you on the outbreak of the Third World War? . . .'

April 15, 1962

Dear Sr. Munoz,

. . . I cannot imagine what *The Times* would say following the outbreak of a nuclear war, but it would certainly be pompous. Perhaps the following might be appropriate. 'While the recent hostilities must be considered regrettable from any point of view, there are yet certain grounds for cautious optimism. The complete destruction of the Soviet Union, together with large areas of Red China, have finally removed the threat of communist subversion from Western Civilisation. The inhabitants of southern New Zealand, Baffin Island, and parts of Tibet may be proud to belong to an alliance of free nations which refused to compromise with the Russian demand that tanks on the Berlin autobahn observe a speed limit of fifty miles an hour. We understand that a number of supporters of Bertrand Russell (Earl Russell) were arrested while demonstrating in the ruins of Montevideo last night. They should realise now what a grave responsibility he bears for weakening Western unity over the past few years. Nevertheless, it must be acknowledged that his contribution in the field of mathematics has been of value. The lesson to be drawn from recent events is that world politics is a sphere best left to men of the calibre of Mr MacMillan and President Kennedy whose joint statement today, issued from the Allied shelter in Antarctica, we cannot improve upon. "The Free World looks out onto a glorious future. Although the United States of America and the United Kingdom, in common with the rest of the Northern Hemisphere, have been completely destroyed, we must warn the Soviet Government that the NATO governments cannot permit the continued provocative flights of Russian planes over the Allied territory of Antarctica. . . ." We trust that the sober warnings of these statesmen will be heeded in New Moscow.'

The sober fact is, however, that a nuclear war would destroy civilisation entirely, and in all probability there would be no survivors whatever. I am enclosing some copies of my most recent speeches, and some leaflets about the Committee of 100, which I hope will interest you.

Yours sincerely
Bertrand Russell

YOUTH AND OLD AGE

FOREWORD

*'I consider old age a time to struggle for human decency—
like any other.'*

Having lived the first twenty-eight years of his life in the nineteenth century, Bertrand Russell rightly claimed 'I may, and
indeed must, reckon myself a Victorian'. Despite reading his own
obituary in 1921 when it was believed he had expired on a visit
to China, and penning another himself which forecast his demise
for 1962, he continued, until his ninety-eighth year, to impress his
presence on the world.

One of the most remarkable facets of his life was his affinity
with young people, whose admiration was more ardent the older
he became. In 1961, when he addressed students at the London
School of Economics, where he had lectured the previous century,
he was able to remark that at a similar meeting held twenty-five
years previously the Chairman was already then referring to him
as a Victorian fossil.

Russell was always conscious that what he had to say is to be
considered and judged by future generations. 'The young are
aware, however remotely, that their elders would have them all
exterminated,' he avers. 'The rebellion of the young is entirely
understandable, and not one iota as irresponsible as the established practices of the old. Denunciation of the young is a form of
excitement suitable to old age and, we may judge, not nearly as
satisfying as that which it condemns.'

To the youth Russell was cast in the mould of a Prometheus. He
passionately opposed authority, convention and dogma—those
respectable ideas which are barriers to human achievement, the
ossification of human curiosity and death to the open mind.
'What is important,' he implored the young, 'is that you preserve
that burning desire to question and challenge accepted views
which is so frightening to the established and so necessary to anything creative or new.' And when the Promethean was threatened
by the gods: 'To defy the stupid, to oppose the malicious is no
easy thing. . . . Be isolated, be ignored, be attacked, be in doubt,

be frightened but do not be silenced.' It is no wonder that Russell was such a potent symbol for today's youth, but he was also an inspiration to the aged, challenging the time-honoured image of old age, retirement and decay. 'One's thoughts must be directed to the future and to things about which there is something to be done,' he wrote in *Portraits from Memory*, and 'I should wish to die while still at work, knowing that others will carry on what I can no longer do, and content that what was possible has been done.'

Russell was concerned to change people's ideas so that they advance their thoughts and actions from the selfish to the social. He saw no dichotomy between youth and age except in those terms and believed that 'A successful old age is easiest for those who have strong impersonal interests involving appropriate activities'. As far as fear of death is concerned, 'the best way to overcome it—so at least it seems to me—is to make your interests gradually wider and more impersonal, until bit by bit the walls of the ego recede, and your life becomes increasingly merged in the universal life'.

Bertrand Russell liked to think of himself as a late survival of a dying age; he outlived all his contemporaries. Nonetheless, he saw humour in this situation, and in a letter to his publisher (Sir Stanley Unwin)[1] refuses to take himself too seriously: '. . . I enclose herewith a postscript to my autobiography as I failed to die when I finished it. If I live to be a hundred, I will send you another.'

[1] Who died in October 1968 at the age of 83.

'. . . Just as a matter of curiosity, what do you feel about old age and do you ever read mystery novels? . . .'

February 9, 1963

Dear Mr Larsen,

Thank you very much for your kind letter. I read many detective novels, and I consider old age a time to struggle for human decency—like any other.

With good wishes,

Yours sincerely
Bertrand Russell

'. . . I have read with great interest the article in the *Manchester Guardian* of your new venture for peace and enclose a small cheque towards the fund. . . . May I say I was in Wormwood Scrubs when you were in the same trouble at Cambridge about 1918–19. I am now rather nearer 89 than 88 and not able to do much. . . .'

October 3, 1963

Dear Mr Griffin,

I was delighted to receive your letter and your generous contribution and wish you to know of my appreciation. I remember very acutely the hectic days of 1918–19 and it pleases me to hear from a comrade and ex-prisoner of that struggle.

With best wishes,

Yours sincerely
Bertrand Russell

'. . . I would like you to know that your birthday and initials are the same as mine! I am going to be 9.

'Happy birthday! . . .'

June 8, 1962

Dear Barbara,

I am very happy to know that my birthday is on the same day as yours and it was interesting to find that we have the same initials.

I am hoping that your birthday was as happy as mine. . . .

Although you are so much younger than I am, I feel that we each have a joy for life which is worth preserving.

With good wishes,

from
Bertrand Russell

'. . . I am an American Student, 13 years old and in the 9th grade . . . In this troubled and turbulent world, with the seeds of unrest all about us, we, the youth of today, look towards men such as yourself for guidance and for perseverance of ideals. The most sinister weapon to come on the horizon of mankind, is the atom bomb. This need not be so, for we have it in our power to harness the atom's energy for peaceful purposes, rather than for warfare. Therefore, we feel we should harness our creative abilities through an education which leads to a peaceful and fruitful life. . . . Since you, as an educator, philosopher, mathematician, and social scientist, have experienced so much in the changing world of the last half century, and because you have been such a courageous and creative man, perhaps you can offer a brief statement on what you think should be the aim of education. . . .'

March 26, 1962

Dear Mark Orfinger,

Thank you for your admirable letter which I read with great interest. I am sorry not to have answered it earlier.

I believe that the main object of education should be to encourage the young to question and to doubt those things which have been taken for granted. What is important is independence of mind. What is bad in education is the unwillingness to permit students to challenge those views which are accepted and those people who are in power. It is necessary for new ideas to emerge, that young people have every encouragement to fundamentally disagree with the stupidities of their day. Most people who are respectable, and most ideas which are considered to be fundamental are barriers to human achievement.

I feel that it is not as important to learn large numbers of things as it is to feel passionately that one has the right to disagree and the obligation to develop new ideas. As you say, our world is troubled and turbulent. All of human civilization is in imminent danger. If there is to be any hope for human beings, all of us must work towards the elimination of these terrible weapons and must think independently about the policies of all of our governments. These governments are preparing murder on a vast scale, and it is necessary for us, the young and the old, to prevent this from taking place.

I am sending to you some statements and if they are of interest to you, I shall be pleased.

With good wishes,

Yours sincerely
Bertrand Russell

'. . . I am 15 yrs. of age and having read several books on Philosophy, have consequently many conflicting views firmly implanted in my own mind. Whenever I try to form my own opinions and reach my own conclusions concerning philosophical matters, I continually find that I am prejudiced and that my reason is being swayed by one or another of these views. This occurs especially when I seem to have reached a "deadlock" in my reasoning or when I have perceived a previous error. I wonder if you could advise me in any way at all on how I might be able to rid my mind of these ideas, some of which, to my mind, contain a high degree of falsity, and be able to think independently. . . .'

March 21, 1962

Dear Mr Rankin,

Thank you very much for your interesting letter, and I am very sorry that I have not answered it before.

I would urge you not to worry about the discovery of conflicting views. Do not resist being swayed by different points of view even if these seem to suggest contradiction. May I encourage you to come to a sympathetic understanding of the position that is being argued. I think you will find that after you have assimilated thoroughly the different philosophical positions, that your own thinking will clarify. It has often been my experience when coming in contact with new ideas that all of them seemed persuasive, and it had only been after I had familiarised myself with them that those things which seemed important became apparent and that which was insignificant became less compelling. It is not error which is a danger to independence of mind. It is unwillingness to question everything. When you come to a point of view, maintain it with doubt. This doubt is precious because it suggests an open mind. I do not mean to argue that we should confuse an open mind with an empty one. I only mean to suggest that truth is an elusive thing, and that certainty is never available to a genuinely enquiring and independent mind.

I am very pleased to see from your letter that you are struggling with ideas for it is this which will lead you to that independence of mind which is creative and worth while.

May I suggest that you read my book: *A History of Western Philosophy*, for I think that the fun I have had with it may appeal to you.

With good wishes,

Yours sincerely
Bertrand Russell

'. . . In the past year or so I've read quite a few general philosophical & scientific works (I'm only 14) . . . it is refreshing indeed to find so rational and lucid an author as you. I'm concerned with many of the topics you write about. As regards education, I wish I could be raised in the ideal schools you've written about. There are precious few of them, but I've heard of one in England at Summerhill, run by A. S. Neill. . . . Last year a Royal Commission on Education put this province [of Canada] a

great step backwards with the reactionary "Chant Report"....
Since you wrote *Marriage and Morals* in 1928, little progress
seems to have been made in morals.... I am Chinese, and regret
it. Belonging to a racial minority is probably harmful.... I haven't
been able to find anybody in any grade who shares my beliefs, or
is even mildly intellectual. If you happen to know anyone
around my age like this, I should certainly appreciate it if you
let me know his address, as I would like to write to him....'

June, 1962

Dear Bob Thing,
... There is one matter about which I feel I must disagree with
you. I spent the years 1920 to 1921 in China and they were
among the most glorious of my life. They were of great importance to me and I believe you would find my book *The Problem of
China* of particular interest. I am appreciative of the meaning of
being a member of a racial minority and I can well imagine the
subtle ways in which you are made to experience indignities every
day. I do not agree that it is harmful to belong to such a minority.
It is difficult, at times, but for people who have independence of
mind and strong character as you have, it provides a perspective
on the follies of the many. You can see that the remarkable
achievement of the Jews is due in no small part to their experience
as a persecuted minority. Obviously, in reality you are a member
of the largest racial group on the planet for one of three human
beings is Chinese. This does not alter the experience you have in
Vancouver.

In your letter to me you say that you have difficulty in finding
someone your own age who shares your intellectual interests. My
granddaughter is exactly your age and, if you wish, she would be
pleased to correspond with you....

With good wishes,

Yours sincerely
Bertrand Russell

'. . . I am drifting—simply drifting. . . . I spend much of my time reading and listening to music. . . . I get so much pure enjoyment from this kind of living, but I know well in my mind that it cannot go on forever . . . and I must go back to work somewhere. I wanted to be a teacher, but I loathe these entrance examinations. I simply cannot recall irrelevant data. I do not have that kind of a mind. . . . What do I do? Work? Go back to school this coming September? Sooner? Do I hide myself from it all, reading and playing the piano? . . . I will have to work—but manual labour is not suited to me; I am not like the others! I like ideas. . . .'

October 8, 1962

Dear Mr Grasse,

Your letter seems to me entirely too occupied with your own private world and rather self-indulgent. I am saying this to you so that you seek some more realistic expression of your desire to do more than vegetate in a retrograde environment.

This requires courage to deal with real problems and to undertake hardship and serious effort in their behalf. If you wish to study, then study and do not moon about wishing to do so. Manual labour is no great tragedy; it is the failure to take oneself less seriously which marks immaturity. I hope you will consider this.

Yours sincerely
Bertrand Russell

'. . . Some time ago I read your Helsinki Speech which appeared to me the best view of a means of gaining approximate World Peace. Perhaps before saying more I ought to tell you that I am 99 and more than half-way through my century year hence senility may make me see things awry. This geophysical year when scientists of some 50 or more nations are contacting each other seems to me the opportunity for putting your suggestions into effect. Why not before the scientists are disbanded hold a geopsychical year. . . .'

September 25, 1957

Dear Miss Jones,

Thank you for your letter of August 17 which reached me only a few days ago. It is nice to receive such a friendly communication from one of your years. I am still fourteen years behind you, but already few of my acquaintances are as old as I am. I like your idea of a geo-psychical year, but I am afraid that, as yet, it would be difficult to get it adopted. I agree with almost everything that you say in your letter.

With best wishes for your approaching centenary,

Yours sincerely
Bertrand Russell

'... I have just celebrated my 100th birthday and have resolved to devote the short time probably left to me of life in working for World Peace.... I would suggest a world-wide meeting at Pekin, Capital of the largest nation in the world, an entirely new environment for politicians, and where all leaders fling aside ambitions and ideologies and work for the common cause of World Peace....'

February 24, 1958

Dear Miss Jones,

Thank you for your letter of February 19. It is comforting and encouraging to learn that after celebrating your hundreth birthday you still have the energy to work for World Peace. As a comparative juvenile, I congratulate you. May you and the World be long preserved to enable you to pursue your beneficent activities! Your idea of a world-wide meeting at Pekin would be admirable if it were feasible, but I am afraid the governmental obstacles are at present insuperable.

Yours truly
Bertrand Russell

Russell comments on a paper entitled 'Medicine and Biology Tomorrow' submitted for his inspection.

March 25, 1957

Dear Dr. Zimmerman,

Thank you for the very interesting paper that you sent me. . . . Your statistics are fascinating and, to me, surprising. I had no idea of the commonness of arterial ailments or of mental disorders.

I think, however, that your practical recommendations as to diet are not very practical. I think that most people, who are not prevented by poverty from over-eating, would prefer a premature death to only one solid meal a day. I am not sure that they would be irrational in this. A completely selfish and completely rational man (if such a man is conceivable) would aim not at long life *per se*, but at the greatest possible balance of pleasure over pain, or, if his circumstances were unfortunate, the smallest possible balance of pain over pleasure—a pain and a pleasure being considered equal when a man is indifferent as to whether he experiences both or neither. I, personally, have succeeded in living nearly eighty-five years without taking any trouble about my diet. But if I had known at twenty that unless I followed your rules I should die at seventy, I hardly think that I should have adopted your precepts. I have no wish to live to 167 like your Colombian Indian. I do not think that I am peculiar in these sentiments. I must add that I think the sort of work contained in your paper is very important, but if it is to have its due effect ways must be found of making recommendations that are not too unpalatable.

Yours sincerely
Bertrand Russell

———————

'. . . A question often asked by my students is, "How important to Bertrand Russell was his high school education, and is college experience necessary for creative writing?" The only answer I have given them so far is to quote from the statement about you in *Twentieth Century Authors*. . . . Is there anything further I could tell my lively students, Lord Bertrand? . . .'

September 18, 1959

Dear Mr Hartley,

. . . As for what your pupils ask you, I had no school education but was taught by tutors until I went to Cambridge. I cannot believe that college experience is necessary for creative writing. Many of the best poets had none and those who had often profited nothing by it—for example, Byron and Shelley. I cannot think of anything further you should tell your 'lively students' except that I am delighted that they are lively. The best source of the information that you may want is Alan Wood's *The Passionate Sceptic* published by Simon & Schuster,[1] which is a biography of me.

Yours sincerely
Bertrand Russell

'. . . Briefly, I am in love with one, Caroline by name, of beauty and intelligence, and, as in the situation which must be all too frequent elsewhere, she does not love me. . . . My reaction to this information was to prepare a poison for my use. . . . A word or two about myself would seem in order. . . . I am twenty years old. . . . I was educated at Bryanston where I did not work from pure laziness and lack of interest . . . and then decided to sit for a scholarship in History to Trinity Coll., Camb. . . . And now Caroline. . . . Why shouldn't I kill myself if I so wish? . . . Why am I going to a university, and further why am I going to read History there? How is this going to help me? . . .'

July 19, 1963

Dear Sir,

. . . May I say that I entirely understand your difficulty. I suggest that you look up Donne's 'When by thy scorn, O murderess, I am dead. . . .', and reflect that after writing this poem the lovelorn poet lived to become Dean of St. Paul's and to preach many eloquent sermons on death.

Unrequited love is like a serious illness—very unpleasant while it lasts but usually not life-long. I should not treat this question as one of morality but as one of rational forecast of your future.

[1] in New York, and by George Allen & Unwin Ltd. in London.

I hope that you will go up to Trinity to read History. It could open a new world to you, and I believe from what you write that you could make the most of this opportunity. Meanwhile, perhaps you might care to write to me a little later to tell me how your preparations for Cambridge are going with your tutor.

With good wishes,

Yours sincerely
Bertrand Russell

'I am very interested to know what your opinions are regarding masturbation. . . . I am tortured mentally by the fact that I have masturbated in the past. . . . I have read that the guilt feelings of a masturbating teenager cannot be explained away, I am sorry and on the verge of suicide. You are my last hope, would you be so kind as to help me in my problems? . . .'

December 24, 1964

Dear Sir,
. . . With regard to masturbation, practically everybody has practised it in adolescence. The theory that it is wicked or harmful is a cruel invention of the old to keep the young in order. Your feelings of guilt are misplaced, since masturbation does nobody any harm.

Yours sincerely
Bertrand Russell

'. . . I and the undersigned are Sixth Form students . . . and we consider ourselves—we hope with some justification—to be open-minded and quite capable of forming our own opinions in conflicting arguments. This, however, is rather difficult when we are given only one side of the argument concerned. We should like to apply this principle to religion, but we are prevented from so doing by archaic public school attitudes in this sphere. Repeated attempts to obtain your book, *Why I am Not a Christian*, which states so clearly the view of the thinking unbeliever, for our school library have failed because of such attitudes. In the interests of free thought we wondered if you would send us an autographed copy of this book, which would solve our problem since the library authorities would hardly refuse a donation of this sort. . . .'

March 18, 1962

Dear Mr Sandbach and Friends,

I am tremendously encouraged to have received your excellent letter. I am afraid that education is conceived more in terms of indoctrination by most school officials than in terms of enlightenment. My own belief is that education must be subversive if it is to be meaningful. By this I mean that it must challenge all the things we take for granted, examine all accepted assumptions, tamper with every sacred cow, and instill a desire to question and doubt. Without this, the mere instruction to memorise data is empty. The attempt to enforce conventional mediocrity on the young is criminal.

So it is greatly rewarding to me to witness your independence of mind. I do not consider it important whether you find yourselves in agreement with any particular point of view. What is important is that you preserve that burning desire to question and challenge accepted views which is so frightening to the established and so necessary to anything creative or new.

I am sending you a copy of *Why I am Not a Christian* with a short inscription inside it. If your school library will not accept it for the use of the school, please keep it yourselves. In fact, I leave to your own preference how you wish to use the book.

With warm good wishes,

Yours sincerely
Bertrand Russell

'. . . While reading your book *The Conquest of Happiness*, specifically chapter nine, "Fear of Public Opinion", I happened, at another moment, upon this [magazine] editorial. . . .

" 'Patriotism has a narrowing effect on people,' wrote Virginia, a straight-A student. 'It confines love to one specific area of land or to one specific set of ideals. . . . It allows an American to love Americans but not Russians and not Communist Chinese. . . . The narrowness of patriotism breeds selfishness and hatred and blindness. . . . Finally this monster of hate and patriotism unleashes war and death and destruction upon the world. . . . Patriotism has outlived its usefulness. . . . It is necessary to replace loyalty to the nation with an even higher loyalty, loyalty to the world. . . .' This eloquent young lady has certainly rung the bell but at the wrong address. It is not patriotism but blind nationalism or chauvinism that is incompatible with a higher loyalty. . . . Our patriotism not only permits us to love both Russians and Chinese, but our consistent dedication to the brotherhood of man demands it. It is the tyrants who enslave them that we abhor. Virginia, like so many others of her generation, is properly troubled by the world's atomic abyss, which makes them uncertain and resentful. . . . But the greater the thermonuclear danger, the more the world needs the rule of law which is the only guarantee of freedom, and which the 'higher loyalty' of American patriots has always espoused."

'. . . I would ask you, sir, a word of encouragement to this young girl. Your thoughts, beliefs and actions are known and admired by many of us; and there is little doubt that if you would you could nullify much of the narrow criticism she is now the brunt of; you could fortify her, help her stay on her course. We need her kind badly. . . .'

March 22, 1962

Dear Virginia,

I should like to take this opportunity to offer to you my deeply felt admiration and gratitude for your courage and for your defence of all that is decent in human experience. I should say to you that to defy the stupid, to oppose the malicious is no easy thing. Continue to speak out. Never forget that your audience is to be measured in generations. You will face persecution and the venom of those who are deaf to man's life and dead to his death.

Be isolated, be ignored, be attacked, be in doubt, be frightened but do not be silenced. What is important in human experience is intellectual independence and creative intelligence. Those . . . who use the noblest sentiments and the best words of our language to justify global butchery, betray human culture and defile human dignity.

As I am writing to you, our planet is covered with rocket bases on a hair trigger. These bases depend on radar which is incapable of distinguishing between natural phenomena and missiles. One of these hydrogen bombs contains more explosive power than twenty million V-2 rockets. The policy of the governments of the United States and Soviet Union is based on a readiness to incinerate human beings in their hundreds of millions. Nuclear war, if present practice continues, is a matter of near certainty.

Neither of these two governments has respect for the intellectual integrity you have shown. Neither of them understands that individual independence of mind is being eliminated by each of them through their intolerance and through their authoritarian contempts for human beings. No political system is so important and no change of regime so intolerable as the mentality which contemplates two out of three human beings alive, living at starvation level; spends $100 million an hour on arms, proudly threatens genocide at every opportunity, and has the colossal arrogance to lay claim to morality and human responsibility.

Keep fast your vision of a more excellent way of life. From across the Atlantic, I offer you my hand.

With all good wishes,

Yours sincerely
Bertrand Russell

'. . . The questionnaire is intended to bring our young readers from the whole world closer to the personal opinions of famous and outstanding persons. . . . We are a Czechoslovak magazine and are trying to make it easier for ordinary people in the whole world who want to live in peace and happiness, to understand one another, to become friends. That is also the purpose of our questionnaire. . . .

'1. If the financial means allocated for armaments were to be made available would you recommend that something special be done for young people?

'2. What do you think is the chief reason why people throughout the world do not understand one another as well as they should?

'3. If you were 20 again what would you do with your life and why?

'4. Do you think you understand the problems of today's young people and that they, in turn, understand you?'

September 16, 1964

Dear Mr Prochazka,

Thank you for your letter of September 14 and for the enclosed questionnaire. I like the magazine that you also sent, which provides a cheerful antidote to gloomy thoughts. I agree heart and soul with the purpose of your magazine and I wish you all success. My answers to the questions in your questionnaire are enclosed.

Yours sincerely
Bertrand Russell

1. I think there are various things that could be done for young people if the expenditure on armaments were abolished. The most obvious of these is education, which might be continued to a later age than is at present common. The quality of the education should be improved by better salaries for teachers and better training colleges for them. The senior classes in schools should have access to laboratories, I think also, medical care for the young could be greatly improved. Another matter which is important, at least in Western countries, is providing paid employment as soon as formal education is finished. For those who have exceptional talents, there should be opportunity of making their skill known by publications specially concerned with work of the young. I think that it would be a good thing if more money were spent in making grants for foreign travel and study.

2. I think there are two chief reasons why people of different countries do not get on with each other. One is difference of language, and the other is the emphasis on nationalism in education. The very young, before they have been subjected to the influence of education have much less difficulty in getting on with people of their own age from another country. They learn each other's languages easily and find the differences amusing rather than shocking. I think that contact with people of other countries in youth is the best way of breaking down national barriers.

3. If I were twenty again, I should set to work to learn physics and chemistry because it is these sciences that are of most importance in the present day. Nuclear physics, in particular, gives us the power of life and death over those whom we choose to regard as enemies. The human race will not long survive unless men with an international outlook are in control of the resources of science.

4. I am often astonished by the understanding and appreciation of my work on the part of the young. I hope that I, in turn, understand their problems, but I do not know how far I succeed in this.

———————

'... I have many acquaintances well over ninety and many between 100 and 150 and others even older in years and younger-looking than your picture shows. I am next door to ninety myself and as healthy and active as when I was fifty. . . .'

June 8, 1962

Dear Dr Carveth,
Thank you for your letter. I had a recent letter, which also interested me, from Methuselah.

Yours sincerely
Bertrand Russell

PHILOSOPHY

FOREWORD

*'. . . I imagine that philosophers will occupy themselves
by studying less and less more and more intently. If they
do this they will be able to survive the ruthless scrutiny of
their governments, if they do not their heads will be removed regardless of the geographical location of the rest
of their bodies.'*

Bertrand Russell always ran the risk of decapitation. Indeed, he
enjoyed relating an anecdote about William, Lord Russell, who
lost his head in 1683 for resisting the restoration of the monarchy.
Like his ancestor he was most reluctant to subscribe to the dictates
of authority, holding firmly to his principles and refusing to
abdicate his social responsibilities.

While Russell insisted on a clear division between his work as a
technical philosopher and his work as a social thinker and man of
action, he was quick to point out that his early achievements would
not enlighten anyone if his opposition to nuclear war failed.

Russell first became well-known as a pioneer of mathematical
logic; later, as a social philosopher, his influence became widespread. He thus likened his life to that of Faust, as being divided
into two distinct periods. The first period occupies the years up
to 1914, during which time Russell set himself the task of dis-
covering whether there was any truth in mathematics. His
magnum opus, *Principia Mathematica*, a joint work with A. N.
Whitehead, was first published in 1910. It was of considerable
bulk, and in a somewhat down-to-earth manner was conveyed
to the publishers in an old horse-drawn carriage. With equal
irreverence it was cast on to a rubbish-dump and burned after
they had done with it, but not before the co-authors had contribu-
ted £50 each to the cost of its publication. Like Einstein's theory
of relativity, the *Principia* is said to be completely understood by
only a few people. Russell, in a letter to two women who assert
their appreciation of the work, insisted: '. . . I cannot believe that
both of you have read *Principia Mathematica*. Hitherto I have
only known of six people who have read it, three Poles who were

liquidated by Hitler, and three Texans, who were absorbed by osmosis into the general population.' Russell dated his second Faustian period from August 1914, and if the *Principia* had a select readership, he was now to aim at the many: 'The First World War diverted my thoughts to matters of more immediate practical moment, from which I was led on to considerations of political and social philosophies', he explained in 'My Own Philosophy', an unpublished 1946 essay.

His first book on social philosophy, *The Principles of Social Reconstruction*, published in 1916, deals with the whole range of problems which would have to be faced in creating a new society. Russell did not stand aloof and remote; he made these social questions the province of Everyman. A debunker of pretentious mystification, he could never be accused of boring the pants off anyone. His works like *Marriage and Morals* and *The Conquest of Happiness* have a wide appeal, and his classical *History of Western Philosophy* is a brilliant account of the philosophy of others. A fifteen-year-old wrote appreciatively, '. . . though some adults think I am too young to understand your books, I find them stimulating and very clear and concise.' Yet Russell never sacrificed the intellectual rigour of his philosophy at the expense of being popularly understood. 'Commercial popularization is not a good thing', he held, 'because it involves distortion through simplification. This is different from making available to people the intellectual world of philosophy which can be done without sacrificing the integrity of the ideas involved. It is a matter of ability and style.' In 1957 he was rewarded with the Kalinga Prize for popularizing science.

This section indicates on the one hand the extent to which Russell related his philosophy of life to the complex problems of living it, and on the other hand his work as a technical philosopher. Many letters he received express the moral dilemmas of his correspondents. In this sense he was often seen by the lay public as an oracle, or a father confessor. But his answers are disarming—no voice could be less God-like than Russell's—advising where he can, admitting ignorance where he cannot.

A reply to one of many letters enquiring which of his works Russell regards as most important.

August 5, 1964

Dear Sir,

Thank you very much for your letter.

If nuclear war is prevented I should consider my opposition to it my most important work. If not, *Principia Mathematica* will not be able to enlighten anyone.

Yours sincerely
Bertrand Russell

. . . the Journal of the Hungarian professionals in the field of engineering sciences turns to the scientists of various countries with the request to express their opinion on the prospective development of the next 20 years in their special field of sciences. We would be greatly honoured if you would communicate to us your views and thoughts in connection with your own field of activities. . . .'

December 31, 1961

Dear Dr Aba,

I am most sorry not to have been able to reply to your letter before now. Since my release from prison because of my activity against nuclear war, I have been overwhelmed with correspondence.

You ask of me whether I would express an opinion on the development of my own field during the next twenty years. I imagine that philosophers will occupy themselves by studying less and less more and more intently. If they do this they will be able to survive the ruthless scrutiny of their governments, if they do not their heads will be removed regardless of the geographical location of the rest of their bodies.

My expectation is that unless philosophers and other ordinary people participate in a movement of resistance against the murderous nuclear policies of the Governments of both West and

East we shall be lucky to be exchanging correspondence in twenty months. I am enclosing some recent statements of the Committee of 100 which is leading a resistance movement against the policies of NATO and of the British Government. I hope you may find them of interest and that you may consider their application to the Warsaw pact. With good wishes,

Yours sincerely
Bertrand Russell

'. . . I am a mathematical logician; we met once at a sherry party. . . . Next week two other logicians are coming to stay for a few days to argue about problems in the foundations of mathematics; I wondered if the three of us might come over, and pay homage to you? . . .'

March 31, 1960

Dear Mr Gandy,
It will be a pleasure to see you and your two fellow logicians on Thursday, April 7, and I suggest that you should come to tea at about four. I am completely out of touch with recent logical work and you will all have to treat me as an ignoramus.

Yours sincerely
Bertrand Russell

'. . . You have been described as a "passionate skeptic". I would like to know the source of your passion. It has not been a religious faith and you have denied being a humanist; then what has been the inspiration for your concern for the rest of us? . . .'

May 24, 1960

Dear Mrs. Stobrawa,
. . . I do not think that I have ever denied being 'a humanist', though I have regretted the abandonment of the older word 'rationalist'. A critic asserted that I was not a humanist because

I did not agree with the philosophy of John Dewey, but I have never thought this an essential part of humanism.

You also ask what is the source of my passion. I do not think that passions have any source. If you saw a child drowning, you would try to save it and would not wait for some -ism to persuade you that it was worth saving. I see the human race drowning and have an equally direct impulse to save it. There is no need to justify this impulse, any more than to justify eating when one is hungry. The -isms by which people attempt to justify their impulses are, in fact, products of the impulses that they pretend to justify.

Yours sincerely
Bertrand Russell

'. . . After reading your recent book, *Bertrand Russell Speaks His Mind*, I am sorry to confess that I am still uncertain what your attitude toward life is. You have taken into consideration the uncertain nature of all things, yet you seem to live life with purpose. I was wondering how you have attained this purposeful attitude not knowing whether everything is determined or whether free will exists? . . .'

February 15, 1963

Dear Mr Barczak,

. . . 'Purpose' is entirely an inner quality which in no way depends upon metaphysical views about causality.

Passionate concern for some degree of understanding of the world outside oneself and compassionate interest in the circumstances of other human beings provide sufficient activity for many lifetimes. Whether this activity is seen to be trivial or considered important is a temperamental accident. I think something may be said for both attitudes, although I act upon the latter one.

Yours sincerely
Bertrand Russell

'. . . I am tracing what I consider to be three of the most important questions in philosophy. These are:
1. What is the purpose of man's existence?
2. How should life be led?
3. In what does happiness consist? . . .'

January 30, 1960

Dear Father Lundmark,
. . . As regards your first question: I do not think man's existence
has any purpose. Purposes can only be assigned to sentient beings
and, therefore, one who does not believe in God can only recognize the individual purposes of separate men and animals. As
regards your second and third questions: you will find all I have
to say in *New Hopes for a Changing World.*

Yours sincerely
Bertrand Russell

'. . . The enclosed paper [is to] be published. . . . I hope it contains
no errors, and that it promotes a new evaluation of your philosophy. . . .'

October 30, 1965

Dear Mrs Eames,
Thank you for your letter . . . and for your article about me, both
of which reached me today. I am grateful for your article and, as
far as I can judge, the things you say about my work are just. I
have always felt, myself, that there is a certain absurdity in criticizing a philosopher for changing his mind as a result of new
scientific work. I think this comes of the many centuries of
association of philosophy with theology. In theology, it is expected that a man should be willing to be burnt at the stake rather
than change his mind. But as philosophy becomes more associated
with science than with theology, a philosopher's opinions should
have a certain flexibility. . . .

Yours sincerely
Bertrand Russell

'. . . In *What I Believe* you put forward the criterion that should underlie moral rules: a human act is "good" if through it the total amount of human happiness increases.

'This supposes however the existence of a measure for human happiness. There are of course cases in which it is easy to decide which of two alternative situations contains most happiness, but the existence of a general standard is not obvious to me.

'In your article "Has Religion made Useful Contributions to Civilisation?" you pretend that the concept of righteousness is a relative one and thus not suitable as a moral standard. However, in the same article you maintain that in the education of children (to prevent jealousy) strict justice is required. I do not see a clear distinction between the concepts of righteousness and justice. . . .'

January 26, 1963

Dear Mr Van Leuven,

 . . . When I say that an act is 'good' if it increases human happiness, I do not imply a general standard for human happiness. I mean to say that 'good' ought to be understood by people as the pursuit of human happiness; as for what constitutes that happiness, that is a matter for continued social debate. We will be wrong and circumstances will alter what is required for human happiness. Nonetheless, the pursuit of it, as we each conceive it to be, is the proper ethical task.

Your second point suggests that the relative nature of 'righteousness' makes 'justice' in the education of children impossible. You will find if you examine the essay that I mean no more than that views of 'righteousness' vary with communities and periods. Justice in the treatment of children is easily understood as the lack of discrimination in the opportunities accorded them and the educational practice of not victimising children with harsh treatment for reasons of pedagogic prejudice. The two ideas ('righteousness') and fair treatment of children seem to be simple ones and not contradictory at all. The entire discussion was a pragmatic one.

Yours sincerely
Bertrand Russell

'I am taking the liberty of presenting you with this copy of my recent book on your moral philosophy. I believe that I have discovered some aspects of your ethical theory that *you* may not even know! At any rate, no one else has written at any length about this area of your philosophy: . . . I started research on this part of your writings primarily because I have always admired you as a philosopher and as a human being. (I think you'll see this from my last chapter.) . . . If you find time to read the book, I would be delighted if you would tell me your opinion. . . .'

August 26, 1963

Dear Professor Aiken,

Many thanks for sending me your book on my ethical doctrines and for the accompanying letter. I have read your book with much interest and have found it invariably accurate in its account of my views. I do not myself think very well of what I have said on ethics. I have suffered a violent conflict between what I felt and what I found myself compelled to believe. This I think you bring out quite fairly. I could not bring myself to think that Auschwitz was wicked only because Hitler was defeated, but the ghosts of Hobbes and the Thrasymachus in the beginning of *The Republic* seemed to jeer at me and say I was 'soft'.

I was a little puzzled by your view that I had made a fundamental change in *Human Society in Ethics and Politics*. I was not conscious of making any such important change. I gather that you do not think much of the idea of compossibility among objects of desire, but I do not quite know why. I am grateful to you for the kind things you say in your last chapter. When you are critical, I think you are generally justified.

Yours sincerely
Bertrand Russell

'. . . I hope you will find time to read [my book] as it deals with your own expression of perplexity which, as you say, you have never glossed over and which all humanists share and you may find one or two suggestions in it by which ethical values may be objectively founded. . . .'

130

June 19, 1960

Dear Mr Osborn,

Thank you for sending me your book *Humanism & Moral Theory*. I have read it with interest, but I regret to say that it has not solved my ethical perplexities. The practical difficulties of ethics were brought forcibly to my notice by an American Army officer, part of whose work during the last war had consisted of trying to persuade Japanese prisoners that it was not their duty to commit suicide. In this, so he assured me, he had had great success and, incidentally, had acquired a liking for the Japanese, which was very rare among Western combatants. But I do not think that it was rational arguments which enabled him to persuade the prisoners. I think it was the effect of a social milieu with different moral attitudes combined with relief at finding an excuse for the instinctive love of life. His account of his experiences led me to wonder what I could have said to a Nazi prisoner if I had wished to persuade him that massacring Jews is not the highest duty of man. I could, of course, have said, 'Well, as you see, it leads to defeat in war.' But I should not have felt this a very adequate argument.

You say, in your book, that ethics is essentially concerned with man as a social being. Personally, I agree with you. But there are those who think differently. For example, Goethe, in *Wilhelm Meister*, sets forth the view that each individual's end should be self-realization, and that this end is best promoted by a combination of masonic mysticism and affairs with housemaids. You and I may disagree with Goethe, but how are we to *prove* that he is wrong?

I cannot see that what you say about psycho-analysis is relevant to the fundamental issue. Psycho-analysis helps us to understand the genesis of people's passions and may show the way of promoting the passions that we like, but it does not show which passions we *ought* to like. I can imagine an argument in favour of the Oedipus complex on the ground that it promotes great achievement. Alexander, for instance, might have remained quiet and obscure if he had not hated his father.

I am sorry to say that your book has only confirmed me in the view that any system of ethics which claims objectivity can only do so by means of a concealed ethical premiss, which, if disputed, cannot be demonstrated.

Yours sincerely
Bertrand Russell

———————

'. . . Do you [think] that it is quite in order to probe . . . into the mathematics and physics of the universe and . . . in doing so find whether it expands or contracts . . . but it is not in order to ask what causes the expansion or contraction? . . .'

April 29, 1959

Dear Sir,
. . . I think it is meaningless to inquire as to the cause of the world. 'Cause' is, in any case, a concept which belongs to a quite out-moded view. In so far as it is applicable at all, we can speak of one occurrence causing another, but this way of speaking is only applicable to bits of the world. To look for a cause of the whole is like trying to define the spatial position of the universe.

Yours truly
Bertrand Russell

———————

'. . . Why do men believe that a human being, whatever he is, is more in the favour of a creator, . . . than an animal? . . .'

September 3, 1952

Dear Mr Luehrs,
The only reason that philosophers think God is more interested in men than in animals is that philosophers are men. Xenophanes who lived in the sixth century B.C. said all that there is to say on this subject: 'Homer and Hesiod have ascribed to the gods all things that are a shame and a disgrace among mortals, stealings

and adulteries and deceivings of one another. . . . Mortals deem that gods are begotten as they are, and have clothes like theirs, and voice and form . . . yes, and if oxen and horses or lions had hands, and could paint with their hands, and produce works of art as men do, horses would paint the forms of gods like horses, and oxen like oxen, and make their bodies in the image of their several kinds. . . . The Ethiopians make their gods black and snub-nosed; the Thracians say theirs have blue eyes and red hair.' The phrase *Homo sapiens* had not been invented in his day. If it had, he would have suggested altering it to *Homo insipiens*, in which he would have had my whole-hearted support.

Yours sincerely
Bertrand Russell

'. . . Last week I was talking to an old man . . . about fox-terriers— I said the one we have is quiet but that I dislike terriers that bark all day long for reasons unknown to me. . . . The old man replied "Well you can put a mirror in front of the dog then he will have something to bark about". . . . I think now that people's ideas about the Universe may be based on the "mirror" idea—Man may be annoyed that he does not know the origin of the Universe and the "mirrors" are all the Religions and "isms". . . . In the future perhaps man will stop basing his life on belonging to clubs—individual churches, villages, countries, and start to find out that there can be not much progression of the spirit or mind until it is freed from the idea of compartments. . . .'

May 24, 1960

Dear Miss Hankinson,
. . . I rather like your old man's suggestion for giving the dog something to bark at. When I was five years old, I kept tame pigeons and, if I put a cock pigeon in front of a mirror, he would peck at it furiously and then run round to the back in hopes of finding this disgusting bird there. The whole incident was very like a meeting of the Big Four.

Social cohesion, which you write about, has a long history. You can read a good account of its origins in Sir Arthur Keith's *New Theory of Human Evolution*. In the past, and still for most people, social cohesion is a tribal affair promoted by fear of a rival tribe. This is what causes the psychological difficulty in advocating a world government. You will find some treatment of this problem in my short book *Authority and the Individual*.

> *Yours sincerely*
> *Bertrand Russell*

'In your book, *The Conquest of Happiness*, in the chapter, "The Sense of Sin", you state that you do not think lying is always unjustified, and you cite the instance in which you were asked by some hunters which way a fox had gone, and you lied to them in order to throw them off the trail and thus spare the exhausted fox's life. Isn't it a fallacy to assume that no adequate, truthful alternative exists in such situations? For instance, couldn't you have said, "Yes, I saw the fox but I'm not going to tell you where it went because I will not be an accomplice to your thoughtless killing." This answer might not throw the hunters off the trail, but it may cause them to think about what they're doing. . . .'

September 28, 1963

Dear Mr Jacobson,

. . . My object was to save the fox. For that purpose it was most effective to mislead the hunters as to the direction taken by the fox. There are many situations, such as those experienced under tyrannies, in which lying may be commendable.

With good wishes,

> *Yours sincerely*
> *Bertrand Russell*

'In this country there is an influential group . . . who denounce what they call Two-Valued Logic. According to these persons, the study of traditional logic promotes unwholesome habits of thinking, which are associated with mental illness, racial prejudice and other evils. They deplore what they call Black-and-White thinking, Either-Or Philosophy and, worst of all Aristotelian Logic. These self-styled non-Aristotelian thinkers sometimes point to you as one of their supporters. Specifically, you are said to endorse *Science and Sanity*, a book in which Alfred Korzybski rejects the laws of Identity, Contradiction and Excluded Middle. . . . I find it hard to believe that you reject the laws of Identity, Contradiction and Excluded Middle. . . .'

May 10, 1958

Dear Dr Angel,

. . . I do not think there is anything wrong with two-valued logic, nor yet with three-valued logic. Each is appropriate for its own class of problems. My criticisms of Aristotelian logic are concerned with details, not with the general conception. I have never admired the work of Korzybski and I do not, in any degree, endorse the supposed connection of Aristotelian logic with mental illness. As for the laws of Identity, Contradiction and Excluded Middle, you will find them all in the early chapters of *Principia Mathematica*.

Yours sincerely
Bertrand Russell

'I have been reading with interest your book *My Philosophical Development*. You say on page 67 that the statement "All Greeks are mortal" cannot be proved by enumeration. The reason given is that this statement in its full form is "For all possible values of x, if x is Greek, x is mortal", and the x in question is not confined to the x's that are Greeks, but extends over the whole universe. I think that "All Greeks are mortal" can nevertheless be proved by enumeration, by putting all Greeks on an island and dropping atom bombs on them for example, and that we may in fact confine our attention to the x's that are Greeks. For suppose x is not Greek. Then the statement "If x is Greek, x is mortal" is true in the same way that "All Lilliputians are mortal" is true. That is, it is true as a matter of logic and not as a matter of observation. Now suppose x is Greek. Then the statement in question can be settled by observation, and since the number of Greeks is finite, that is by enumeration.

November 14, 1964

Dear Mr Thompson,

. . . The reply to your contention is that no enumeration can make certain that you have enumerated *all* the Greeks. There may be Greeks in the Gobi Desert descended from Alexander's army. There may be Greeks who live under ground and have never been discovered. Such possibilities are unlikely, but not impossible. The statement 'All Greeks are mortal' may be stated as 'there is nothing which is an immortal Greek'. This is a statement about everything in the world. Your suggestion of collecting all Greeks and putting them on an island assumes there are no Greeks unknown to you. This may be true, but cannot be demonstrated without a survey of the whole universe.

Yours sincerely
Bertrand Russell

'. . . Can man truly desire evil? . . .'

October 16, 1962

Dear Miss Colodner,

. . . With regard to your question about man truly desiring evil, the problem is one of examining the way in which 'evil' is used in your sentence. If 'evil' is intended to mean such things as are undesirable, the answer to your question is obviously 'No'. But this is a trivial truth. If 'evil' is meant to refer to those things which the desirer feels disapproval, then it is perfectly possible for 'evil' to be desired.

The problem is that no objective criteria are available to tell us that things are 'evil' or 'good'. Such words serve to show how we feel about things and how we wish to have them considered. I should feel cruelty and mass murder to be evil and I should wish for others to consider them as I do. This does not preclude any-one from desiring both cruelty and mass murder as the behaviour of all men of power and the majority of mankind suggests.

Yours sincerely
Bertrand Russell

'. . . Just what is your position in relation to the question of determinism vs. free-will? . . .'

January 14, 1957

Dear Mr Davidson,

The question of determinism and free will is a difficult one and I am not completely satisfied either with my own views or with anyone else's. You will find a discussion of it in a book of mine which in America is called *Scientific Method in Philosophy*, but in England is called *Our Knowledge of the External World*. The last chapter in this book says all that I have to say on deter-minism and free will. If you find the discussion unsatisfactory, I can only say that I agree with you.

Yours sincerely
Bertrand Russell

'This is a letter from an unknown Indian youth who reads your books with deep interest. . . . Is knowledge at all possible? in the ultimate analysis, we have two sources of knowledge, viz. intellect and senses. But can either of them be considered as capable of conveying objective knowledge? So far as our senses are con-cerned, they are extremely individual in character. And the intellect with which we try to understand our sense-data is also the intellect of the individual. How, then, objective knowledge is possible? It may be argued that if there is general agreement on a particular point, it may be considered as objective knowledge. But very often widely accepted universal opinions have been contradicted later on. Thus it seems that we are always in a world of probable, and not certain, knowledge, which only approximates truth. Moreover, even where there is a concensus of opinion, how can we know, that two persons are really holding the same opinion? Suppose, I say "Grass is green", and another person agrees. But how can I know that he means exactly the same things as I do when I use the two words "grass" and "green"? Here, of course, comes the difficulty about language. Is language a perfect medium of expression? . . .'

October 20, 1962

Dear Mr Choudhury,

. . . The quest for objective knowledge is to be found either in the certainties of mathematics wherein, because the system is closed and without reference to the external world, knowledge is definite, or in the world of experience when public criteria have been agreed upon. The latter entails what is known as scientific method.

Such knowledge as is to be gained from the empirical world is tentative because it can be, in principle, always controverted. Were this not possible then such knowledge would be of small value for it would be impossible to locate what kind of evidence served to support it since none could be said to possibly refute it. The tentative character of scientific knowledge does not compromise its objectivity if one is prepared to modify in the light of evidence which requires this.

The desire to have knowledge which can not be challenged, the certainty of final truth is not likely to lead so much to objectivity as to rigidity and arrogant dogma.

In your example of one man maintaining 'grass is green' the agreement elicited from another can be assumed to mean the same to the second person by observing whether other usages of 'green' and of 'grass' on his part correspond to one's own. It is then reasonable to conclude that each mean the same by the same expression and such an assumption makes further social intercourse more feasible. Naturally, when the day arrives that 'grass is green' brings forth behaviour suggesting that the user has a different understanding of these words than you assume, it should be worth questioning the previously assumed correspondence. These are not matters of certainty, as I have tried to suggest above, but matters of consensus, the departure from which should derive from newly experienced evidence. No other knowledge is available to us.

Yours sincerely
Bertrand Russell

'. . . we have been discussing your book *Problems of Philosophy* and, in particular, the distinction drawn by you between "Knowledge by acquaintance" and "Knowledge by description" and I have been trying to see exactly what you, yourself, intend in this distinction. . . .'

June 16, 1960

Dear Miss Bransby,
. . . The distinction between knowledge by acquaintance and knowledge by description is quite simple whatever other people may have tried to make you think. A single word of which you know the meaning through having what it means wordlessly pointed out to you is one designating knowledge by acquaintance. This includes all the commonest nouns, such as eye, and nose, and cat and dog, and also includes the proper names of people whom you know. Knowledge by description, on the other hand, requires a phrase consisting of several words, none of them, separately, pointing to a definite object, but, taken altogether, sometimes indicating something. Take, say, 'the tallest man in the United States'. Probably no one knows who he is, but there is no doubt a definite man to whom this description is applicable. Many descriptions, however, though correct in form, are not applicable to anything. For instance, 'the tallest man on the top of Everest at the present moment'. . . .

Yours sincerely
Bertrand Russell

Questions from the editors of a Yugoslav journal:

'. . . 1. We would like to know your opinion about the defining property and the constituent parts of philosophy. . . .

2. . . . what role, if any, belongs to philosophy in transforming the world and creating a better future for mankind?

3. Which of your published works do you regard as the most adequate expression of your present views, and which of them do you regard as the most valuable contribution to philosophy? . . .

4. What is your opinion about contemporary philosophical thought in Great Britain? . . . How do you like Wittgenstein's "Philosophical Investigations" and "Remarks on the Foundations of Mathematics"? . . .

5. How do you estimate . . . the existentialist philosophy of Martin Heidegger, Karl Jaspers and J-P. Sartre?

6. What is your opinion about the value of Marxist philosophy? . . .

7. Do you consider a fair discussion between the representatives of different contemporary philosophical schools and currents possible and desirable?

8. Would you like to add . . . some special word for your Yugoslav readers? . . .'

May 27, 1957

Dear Mr Petrovic and Mr Tanovic,

Some of the questions that you ask me can only be answered at considerable length. When this is the case, I will refer you to published articles.

1. What I have to say about the definition of 'philosophy' I have said at the beginning of my *History of Western Philosophy*.

2. I do not think the world will be transformed by philosophy. All that philosophy can do is to generate a comprehensive vision and mitigate the acerbity of dogmatic disagreement.

3. The most adequate expression of my *theoretical* view is *Human Knowledge: its Scope & Limits*. In political theory I should place first my book *Power*; as regards political practice, I should commend *Human Society in Ethics & Politics*.

4. I am not in agreement with much of contemporary British

philosophy. I think that philosophy, like science, should aim at agreement with *fact* and cannot treat language as autonomous. I do not like Wittgenstein's later writings. The present-day English philosopher of whom I think best is A. J. Ayer.

5. I think the Existentialist philosophy is pure nonsense, based intellectually upon errors of syntax and emotionally upon exasperation.

6. You will find my opinions on Marx in the relevant chapters of *Freedom and Organization*.

7. I certainly think that a fair discussion by representative philosophical schools is possible and desirable. I have participated in such discussions myself at international congresses.

8. The only thing that I have to say specially for Yugoslav readers is that one of the chief dangers of the contemporary world arises from the crystallization of opinion into two opposite orthodoxies and that anything on either side which softens the hardness of the creed is so much to the good.

Yours sincerely
Bertrand Russell

'I am an Italian boy of 23 and I am studying Political Science at the University. . . . I should be greatly indebted to You if You can give me the outlines of Your political thought. . . .'

October 21, 1962

Dear Sr. Monforte,

. . . I can not give you an outline of my political thought in a letter except in rather superficial terms. I should wish to see the maximum encouragement of independent thought in any society for I believe that creative things beneficial to mankind emerge only from self-sufficient individuals who pursue knowledge without regard to the susceptibilities of authority or the weight of convention.

I should hope that such a society would provide for the material welfare of all its citizens, that the degree of organisation would be only such as to make stable life feasible and that all members of that society would be encouraged to participate in the public policy of it.

The values of such a community would centre around the provision of occupation for people which proved to be coincident with their joy. Work ought not to be something from which people derive no creative satisfaction and, therefore, experience as drudgery. The social units should be small and a federal principle should obtain between different units. Cultural diversity among the communities should be valued and world organisation should have this as a major consideration. In this way the necessity for world order to cope with natural problems would not be incompatible with open societies and political and cultural freedom.

Naturally, this is a vision which does not correspond with the world around us. I believe that individual conscience must guide men to make sacrifices on behalf of such a vision. It may appear as a distant hope today, particularly when so much energy is devoted to mutual harm and for destruction. I believe, despite this, that man is capable of such a way of life and, I should hope, that young people like yourself would consider the sacrifice of working towards it worthwhile.

Yours sincerely
Bertrand Russell

'I have recently read your book *Political Ideals*. . . . In reference to the part concerning "Pitfalls in Socialism", could you please answer the following questions?

1. What brand of socialism do you criticize when you say that such a system can deprive the individual of liberty?

2. Wouldn't a democratic constitution keep in check an elected assembly representing all industries and having a centralized control over the national economy? . . .'

July 3, 1964

Dear Mr Muller,
. . . The danger of liberty involved in almost any form of socialism comes from the power of officials. If socialism is to permit free-

dom, powerful officials must somehow be curbed, for, if not, they will inherit all the powers of capitalists. I think that something along the lines of Guild Socialism would be the best answer. A democratic constitution is not necessarily a safeguard if the democratic control is somewhat distant. For example, if the Prime Minister were democratically elected and had the power of appointing and dismissing officials, the democratic control would disappear except in the case of very important officials. I am sorry to be so brief, but I am overwhelmed with work.

Yours sincerely
Bertrand Russell

───────────

'. . . I understand from *Which Way to Peace?* that you were then an absolute Pacifist. I understand that Hitler's inhuman regime changed your views. Now I presume that even though another Hitler should arise you would Now revert to Absolute Pacifism because of the power of atomic weapons. . . . Now I want to suggest, that perhaps you have . . . never experienced the emotional circumstances which, if you had experienced them, might have modified your reasoning in 1939. I am suggesting that your reasoning was, of necessity, cold; that had you been at some time in direct contact with, say, bomb-mutilated women and children, you would have remained an Absolute Pacifist. . . .'

October 12, 1956

Dear Sir,

. . . I have never been an absolute pacifist or an absolute anything else. I think that an act is to be judged right or wrong by its consequences: the right act being that which of all acts that are possible gives the greatest balance of good over bad consequences. General rules, such as 'Do not steal' and 'Do not kill', are right in the great majority of cases, but are liable to exceptions.

You ask whether I have ever been in contact with prolonged suffering of innocent people caused by war. I have not. I might retort: have you ever been at Auschwitz and watched large numbers of innocent Jews herded into the gas chamber? If you have not, then, to quote your own phrase, 'your reasoning is of necessity cold'.

> Yours truly
> Bertrand Russell

'. . . For world peace . . . the nations with the exception of *Israel* [should] disarm. . . . That *Israel* guard peace with atomic-bases in all states and man-power from *Israel*. . . . That the United Nations move to Jerusalem, and there enter an alliance—*The League of Israel*— . . . no lasting peace can be obtained unless there is a strong force to guard peace. This guardianship can not be given to anybody, but only to people who have shewn themselves lovers of peace. . . .'

> December 28, 1961

Dear Sir,

Thank you for your letter. I am afraid that I cannot agree that any particular people are especially suited to solve all men's woes or to supervise his conduct. It is because of my intense conviction that such a belief is likely to wreak havoc that I passionately opposed the Nazis from the moment of their formation.

> Yours sincerely
> Bertrand Russell

'. . . Our Class is discussing Communism. . . . Under your theory we would like to know:

1. Should we force the individual who doesn't want Communism to accept it?

2. Were the lives lost and the wars fought in the fight for democracy in vain?

3. Which Communism do you advocate, Russian or Marxian?

4. Would your Communistic ideas turn into a second "1984"?

5. Would this result in world wide equality or slavery? . . .'

May 19, 1959

Dear Carole Kutner,

Thank you for your letter of May 11. I judge from it that you have been completely misled as to my attitude towards Communism. I published a book, *The Practice and Theory of Bolshevism*, against it in 1920 which was reprinted a few years ago. I criticized the doctrines of Marx in 1896 in my first published book, *German Social Democracy*. I criticized him again in *Freedom and Organization* (1934). You will find an article called 'Why I am not a Communist' in *Portraits from Memory* (1956). In short, I am not and never have been a Communist.

I have been urging recently that, in view of the destructive character of the H-bomb, a world war would now be a catastrophe to mankind. Warmongers have countered my propaganda by pretending that I am a Communist.

Yours truly
Bertrand Russell

———————

'. . . As a student of philosophy, I find it almost imperative that I deny the existence of true freedom. . . . To be red or dead? The first is the most obviously lesser evil. But as I wrote [to] that fellow Arizonan and countryman of mine, Barry Morris Goldwater "If Communist domination or human destruction are mankind's only hopes, then I say that freedom has long since died. Choice between two deaths is not choice but coercion. Let us choose life free from both." But realistically I acknowledge the nonexistence of this choice. . . .'

July 24, 1962

Dear Mr Fields,

. . . As to the alternative 'Red or Dead', it is a quite unreal one. It would be perfectly easy, if the West so desired, to reach an accommodation leaving part of the world Communist and part Capitalist, and letting semanticism debate the amount of freedom in either and whether it is greater on one side than on the other.

More generally, *complete* freedom is incompatible with organized society, but the amount of freedom that is possible in any given community depends upon how much tolerance there is in the general outlook. Byzantines could not tolerate even the minutest heresy as regards the Trinity. Some more or less modern communities have difficulty in tolerating atheism. White men in New Zealand are completely tolerant of Maoris, but in many parts of the world such tolerance is found impossible. I think the whole question of freedom must be treated in relation to some given community and answered differently according to the varying temper of different places and times.

> *Yours sincerely*
> *Bertrand Russell*

'I have read your *Marriage and Morals* and *Unpopular Essays*. I am fifteen; and though some adults think I am too young to understand your books, I find them stimulating and very clear and concise. I would like to ask you four questions. First, do you still consider the Negroes an inferior race, as you did when you wrote *Marriage and Morals*? Second, how do the sexual attitudes and education of my generation compare with those of the last? Third, I want to be a writer; what is the best way to learn how to do this? . . . Fourth, assuming your answer to my first question is "no", what do you think of the current civil rights movement in the United States? . . .'

March 17, 1964

Dear Miss Dorheim,

Thank you for your interesting letter. I should answer your questions as follows:

1. I never held Negroes to be inherently inferior. The statement in *Marriage and Morals* refers to environmental conditioning. I have had it withdrawn from subsequent editions because it is clearly ambiguous.

2. The sexual attitudes of your generation seem to me more healthy than those of my own. There is, still, considerable hypo-

crisy and cruelty, but less than in recent times. Our attitudes to sexual freedom are more intelligent, although homosexuality and sexual eccentricities are still treated with abhorrence which has no justification.

3. The best way to learn to write is to read and to write considerably.

4. I entirely approve the civil rights movement in the United States and hope it will increase in momentum and militance.

Yours sincerely
Bertrand Russell

'. . . I hope you will forgive me for this enquiry about a passage, in one of your [books]. It was a discussion about the common human fear of losing one's personal identity after death. And you suggested that this fear was unreasonable in view of the fact that few of us are dismayed by the thought that we have not existed *before* birth. This is putting it very crudely and badly, but I do remember being greatly impressed by the thought "Not to exist" appals us. . . . "Not to have existed" does not. . . .'

August 25, 1959

Dear Mr Nichols,
. . . I am very sorry that I cannot remember in what book the passage occurs that you write about. The question at issue is part of the larger irrationality that we mind unpleasant things in the future more than in the past, which is why people like stories to have a happy ending.

Yours sincerely
Bertrand Russell

'. . . Can you offer a justification for the giving of life which is free from the taint of self-interest? In other words, can we excuse ourselves to our offspring without laying ourselves open to an accusation of having done something which might, in a variety of ways, please ourselves but which from our own experience of living, we know beforehand might give little pleasure to them? . . .'

October 21, 1964

Dear Mr Cumming,
. . . The question with which your letter is concerned is one which is easy to answer in the abstract, but not so easy in the concrete. In the abstract, the scheme is as follows: you enumerate all the possible consequences that may occur if the hypothetical child exists and then all those that may occur if he does not exist. To each of these you attach the probability of its occurrence. You then add up all the good occurrences which are bound up with his existence and subtract all the bad occurrences, using the principle that a good and an evil are to be considered equal if you are indifferent whether you have both or neither. If the result is positive, the child's life is worth while; if negative, it is not. As a refinement, you can go through the same calculation on the assumption of his non-existence, and, in that case, you will conclude that his existence is desirable if the sum of the consequences of his existence is greater than that of his non-existence.

But all this is abstract, and is not much help in practice. In practice people differ in their estimate of goods and evils, and the possibility of knowing what effects a hitherto unborn child will have is very small.

In practice, I should say, that, if a child seems likely to have a happy life, one does nothing wrong in bringing about its existence. The view you suggest—namely, that to bring a child into the world is a sinful act—is only justifiable on the assumption that most human lives are unhappy. I very much doubt whether this is the case even in the present nuclear age, and therefore, I should not condemn a parent save in exceptional circumstances.

Yours sincerely
Bertrand Russell

'. . . 1. Do you think sexual education is necessary?
  2. If so, who is to carry it out? The parents? or the teachers?
  3. At what age is it to begin?
  4. Do you approve of the methods usually advocated?
  5. Do you consider that the mixed school (boys and girls together) helps or impedes sexual education?
  6. Are not we making too much of sex? . . .'

August 15, 1951

Dear Mr Dauven,

  . . . I have had a fair amount of experience of the sexual education of children, first with my own children, second with very young children in a school which I kept at one time, and third with the children of my friends. I think there is no difficulty whatever in the question of sexual education except in the inhibitions of adults. I will take your questions in order.

  1. Is sexual education necessary? Certainly it is. Children left to themselves acquire sexual knowledge from the dirty talk of other children which is at once inaccurate and obscene. This is not the best way to acquire sexual knowledge. Parents invariably forget their own youth and imagine that if they tell their children nothing about sex their children will know nothing about it.

  2. Who is to give sexual education? If the parents are capable of sanity in matters of sex, they should give it. But most parents are of opinion that there is something shameful about the method by which they have brought their children into the world, and so long as they feel in that way, the instruction should be given by teachers.

  3. At what age? This depends partly upon the intelligence of the children. The only thing of importance is that sexual education should be finished before puberty, since at that early time it can be apprehended in a less emotional manner than is possible later on.

  4. I do not know what methods are usually advocated. The right method is to treat sexual matters exactly as one treats all other matters. Whenever the child expresses curiosity, his or her question should be answered with whatever degree of fullness he or she may at the moment desire. I do not think sexual knowledge

149

should be thrust upon children as the multiplication table is. I think it should be given in response to their curiosity.

5. I think mixed schools are a help in sexual education, provided parents and teachers can eliminate prudery from their feelings and behaviour.

6. You ask are we making too much of sex? I am certainly of opinion that those who entertain old-fashioned views make much too much of it. They think it so important that it is worth while to cramp the intelligence and distort the emotions of the young, and to cause them to be obsessed by sex to a wholly unnatural degree. This is the inevitable result of conventional methods. When there is freedom, sex takes its due place and ceases to be an obsessional madness as with St Anthony.

Yours truly
Bertrand Russell

'. . . Do you still feel that married people can live happily together and raise stable children in the manner you prescribed in 1929 (in the Bantam Books edition of *Marriage and Morals*). . . . Or is it possible that your ideas have changed somewhat during the past thirty years? . . . my wife believes in your philosophy and would like our marriage to continue on that basis. . . . I disagree on this point of a happy marriage with both parties having extra-marital sexual relations. Neither of us want a divorce because we both love the children very much. . . .'

June 10, 1959

Dear Sir,
. . . I have not got the edition of *Marriage and Morals* to which you refer, but I think I know the purport of the question that you ask. I have not at present any very decided opinion. What I incline to think is roughly as follows:

A marriage has much greater chances of happiness if both parties are faithful than if one or both are not. At the same time, where a strong affection survives between husband and wife, I think it should be possible for the marriage to remain valuable in spite of infidelities. Individuals differ enormously in the degree to which jealousy makes good relations impossible, and for this reason, I do not think that one can make general rules. I think the question whether a marriage should be preserved for the sake of the children depends upon the degree of friendliness between the parents. If they hate each other and are apt to quarrel, I think a divorce is better for the children, but if they can preserve friendly relations, it is usually better to keep the marriage in being. I think, however, that when the husband or the wife feels a very deep and very overwhelming love for another person, there may be so much harm in resisting it as to outweigh any possible good.

I am afraid all this is somewhat vague and tentative, but I cannot, with full conviction, say anything more definite.

Yours truly
Bertrand Russell

'... I have been happily married for the last 23 years and have 5 children ages ranging from 8 to 21 years. About two years ago, my wife began a homosexual relationship. . . . This . . . relationship is justified amongst other things by my wife, on the grounds of your writings *Why I am Not a Christian* page 55, where you state—"It should be recognised that, in the absence of children sexual relations are a purely private matter which does not concern either the state or the neighbours. Certain forms of sex which do not lead to children are at present punished by the Criminal Law. This is purely superstitious since the matter is one which affects no-one except the parties directly concerned."
. . . I personally believe that your intentions have been completely misinterpreted. May I ask you, therefore, the following questions:—

1. In the circumstances abovementioned, is homosexuality a matter only for the two people immediately concerned?

2. If so, what about the happiness of the other members of the two families?

3. On page 209, you say—"Marriage is the best and most important relation that can exist between two human beings."

Shouldn't the relationship of marriage between man and woman override any relationship between two women?

4. In your opinion is homosexuality morally justifiable in the circumstances mentioned above? . . .'

November 24, 1959

Dear Sir,

. . . My attitude about homosexuality is that it should be regarded no differently from heterosexual relations. When I say that it is a matter only for the people immediately concerned, I should certainly include a husband or wife as immediately concerned; and the children also, obviously are concerned. Very often these family considerations would make extra-marital homosexual or heterosexual relations undesirable, but, if one party to a marriage is deeply and seriously in love with someone else, it is hardly possible for the marriage to remain happy, and sometimes divorce would be best. One cannot make general rules in such matters.

Yours sincerely
Bertrand Russell

'. . . A few weeks ago I read your book, *Marriage & Morals*. . . . On premarital relations do you agree with the following?

1. It's nothing to be ashamed of & it's OK if you're in love but it's like opening your Xmas present in October.

2. It's too difficult to distinguish at an early age the feeling of love from sexual attraction. . . . '

April 6, 1964

Dear Mr Davidoff,

. . . I do not entirely agree with the two points you mention. Sex is a need and does not require intense love for its gratification. Attraction is sufficient if contraception is understood and used. Love is more rare, but will occur in time. Abstinence only provides inexperience and later difficulty.

Yours sincerely
Bertrand Russell

'I have lately been re-reading your book *The Conquest of Happiness*. One statement in it stimulated my curiosity: . . . "It is a peculiarity of modern communities that they are divided into sets which differ profoundly in their morals and in their beliefs. This state of affairs began with the Reformation, or perhaps one should say with the Renaissance, and has grown more pronounced ever since." . . . I would be most indebted to you if you could refer me to material which would tend to substantiate this idea. Of course it would be quite a feat on your part to remember something you referred to thirty years ago. . . .'

May 16, 1960

Dear Mr Gardner,

. . . I do not know exactly what to offer you in the way of 'material' to substantiate the diversity within a modern community. I should have thought this was obvious to any observer. I can give you one illustration. You may remember that in 1940 I was deprived of a professorship in the College of the City of New York on account of opinions which I had expressed in a book called *Marriage & Morals*. Just before this happened, I got a letter from a young American saying, in effect, 'Why do you keep on saying things about sexual ethics which now-a-days everybody agrees with and which, therefore, are not worth saying?'

Yours truly
Bertrand Russell

———

'The author of this treatise—that I enclose—was my fiancé . . . he died in a car crash in which I was slightly injured. He was 24 years old. . . . As my destiny was to live, I will devote all my life to make his ideas known in the world of thought. His life was short, but I am certain that his name will live. I beg you to read this paper carefully. . . .'

July 15, 1959

Dear Miss Notari,

Thank you for your letter and for the typescript by your late fiancé. You have my deepest sympathy in your loss and, from the typescript that you sent me, I should judge that he had considerable philosophical ability. I cannot altogether agree with his thesis as I think that he treats *possibility* as something more substantial than it seems to me, but one cannot judge of philosophical merit by whether one agrees or disagrees with the opinions expressed.

As regards possible publication, I am afraid that I am not the best person to help you. It will certainly be difficult to get your fiancé's work published; and, if this is to be done, you will need someone more in the swim than I am. It is possible that Professor A. J. Ayer at Oxford might be able to assist you, but whether he would do so would, of course, depend upon his estimate of the philosophical merit of the typescript. My own estimate is that, while it shows much promise and gives every reason to think that your fiancé might have achieved something important, it is, as one might expect from so young a man, somewhat immature. I find it difficult to judge what estimate other philosophers would make of it.

The only other name that I can think of, in addition to that of Professor Ayer, is that of Professor Paul Weiss of Yale University who is the editor of a philosophical magazine called *The Review of Metaphysics*. I think either Ayer or Weiss could, at least, tell you what would be the best steps to take and I hope you will have some success.

I return the typescript herewith.

Yours sincerely
Bertrand Russell

'. . . I disagree with you on your reasoning that traditional philosophy is a decaying force in the modern world as mentioned in your book *Our Knowledge of the External World*. Your position as I understand it is that in an atomic age we should discard vague generalities and substitute results which are specific, detailed and verifiable. Isn't it true though, that Dr. Albert Einstein began his Relativity Theory concerning the nature of matter, with a "generality" or hypothesis, . . . and proceeded thus to prove its validity logically and mathematically. . . . Isn't it true as a matter of fact that all great or practically all great philosophical and scientific achievements had their "root beginnings" in a vague generality. . . . You mentioned in your book *Bertrand Russell Speaks his Mind* that while at Princeton, New Jersey, you used to drop in and see and talk with Dr. Einstein once or twice a week and other eminent German Jews on the fundamentals in philosophy and you mentioned that you stood for "hardheaded empiricism" and they stood for "a certain kind of mystical idealism" and that you and Einstein could never seem to cross this gulf that separated you and he. Please if possible describe in detail what you mean by "mystical idealism"? . . . I am what you would term as being a "strong individualist". As you are probably aware, in this country anyone who proclaims to be an "individualist" is immediately sneered at or "mocked" as being a communist or a traitor to his country. . . .'

March 19, 1962

Dear Mr Fuller,

Thank you for your interesting letter. By vague generalities, I do not mean scientific hypotheses, which can in principle be submitted to empirical evidence for testing. I mean rather, vague statements, the terms of which are so unclear as to seem profound but, in fact, provide no more profundity than confusion permits. I certainly agree that individual sensibility and intellectual independence are vital qualities for any creative individual or worthwhile civilization. I agree that the United States is showing itself in total contempt of these qualities and because of this, I believe America to be a dangerous and destructive force in world affairs.

My experience with Albert Einstein was an intense and entirely warm one. His sense of a mystic or intuitive order in the universe was not one I could entirely share, although our estimates of what is important in human experience were close indeed. I certainly agree with him that there is objective truth ascertainable to human intelligence, and that the drama of seeking this is the noblest endeavour available to men. Thank you for writing.

With good wishes,

Yours sincerely
Bertrand Russell

'It is often said that Frege's work was completely overlooked until you drew attention to it in 1903. I have written a paper to show that Peano often referred to Frege's work, before 1901. What, I think, people should say is that you were the first to appreciate the exceptional *importance* of Frege's work. . . .'

February 2, 1961

Dear Professor Nidditch,

. . . I first became aware of the existence of Frege through a review of him by Peano (I think in the *Revista Mathematica*) which censured him for undue subtlety. As Peano was the subtlest logician that I had so far come across, this whetted my curiosity and I got hold of all Frege's books. I am pretty sure that I have mentioned this somewhere in print, but I have not succeeded in finding the passage that I seem to remember. I know, however, quite definitely, that it was through Peano that I first became aware of Frege's existence.

Yours sincerely
Bertrand Russell

'. . . I liked your recommendation of some essential contributions to mathematical infinity. May I mention one of the finest pieces of work in this field, written by your old friend Louis Couturat, entitled *De l'Infini Mathématique*. He published it in 1896, that is one year before you published your book *An Essay on the Foundations of Geometry* . . . [also] did you know Henri Poincaré? . . . What sort of a man was he? . . .'

August 16, 1958

Dear Professor Yourgrau,

. . . As regards Couturat, I reviewed his book *De l'Infini Mathématique* in *Mind* for 1897. This review led to a friendship which lasted till his death.

I knew Henri Poincaré slightly. We had two controversies: the first, about non-Euclidean geometry, in which he was right and I was wrong; the second, about mathematical induction, which he regarded as a principle of inference and I regarded as the definition of 'finite number'. In this second controversy, I was right and he was wrong. He was a very able man, and also witty. I enjoyed his jibe: 'Logistic is no longer sterile. It begets contradiction.' But I think his philosophy was vitiated by an admiration for Kant.

Yours very sincerely
Bertrand Russell

'. . . On reading your *Western Philosophy*—I find that your only references to Pascal are in the spirit of unkind (almost savage) dismissal—even though his mathematical genius might reasonably be compared with your own. Could you tell me, Sir, if you have ever written or spoken on the subject of Pascal, and if so, where I should find this in print? . . .'

July 17, 1956

Dear Mr Cosstick,
. . . As regards Pascal, I took great interest in him during adolescence and, when an aunt of mine offered me a choice of birthday presents, I chose his *Pensées*, which she gave me in a very fine edition. I came later, however, to think exceedingly ill of him. I find in him the source of much of the sentimentalism of the Romantic Movement, and in general, of the rebellion against reason which has disfigured much philosophizing ever since Rousseau. I have never written on Pascal specifically, but, if I did, what I should say would be not unlike what I have said of Rousseau.

Yours truly
Bertrand Russell

'. . . It is clear that in his early phase Wittgenstein felt the need of a special language designed for the use of philosophers somewhat as the symbolism of *Principia* was designed for the use of logicians. I think it is implicit in the outlook of his later phase that he would not have attached importance to any such device. It is not clear from my reading whether you would once upon a time have thought the creation of an artificial language designed for philosophers a useful device and, if so, whether you would still feel it useful or whether you would have changed your mind by now, as I think Wittgenstein did. . . . I find the later work of Wittgenstein terribly disappointing. He seems to wander around the minutiae of linguistics and to preoccupy himself with matters which are the trivia of anyone who is reasonably polyglot.'

October 12, 1959

Dear Sir,

Thank you for your letter of October 8. I am very pleased that your opinion of Wittgenstein's later work is the same as mine.

As regards the question of a philosophical language, I still think that some departures from colloquial language would help philosophers to think more clearly than they do. To take one point: the philosophy of time is bedevilled by the fact that verbs have tense; it is very difficult in ordinary language to express the fact of Brutus killing Caesar without indicating whether this fact is past, present or future. The word 'is' can be used timelessly, as in 'honesty is the best policy' or 'four is twice two', but there is no simple way of stating that Brutus killing Caesar is, in a timeless sense, part of the constitution of the universe. Philosophers puzzle themselves by observing that the past does not exist and the future does not exist, and fail to observe that they are the slaves of a linguistic defect. Or, take again, E upside down which I dealt with in the section called 'Logic and Ontology', at the end of *My Philosophical Development*. It is inconvenient that ordinary language possesses no straightforward way of expressing this idea.

There is another way in which I think that the idea of a philosophical language may be important, and that is as regards minimum vocabularies. The question: 'What is the smallest store of undefined words in which our knowledge can be expressed' is one that seems to me important. But I am not anxious that a philosophical language should be actually employed except for the purpose of a small number of problems.

It is a long time since I came to these opinions and I do not think that they were much influenced by Wittgenstein.

With kind regards,

Yours sincerely
Bertrand Russell

'. . . do you know if Whitehead ever read Wittgenstein? . . .'

January 26, 1963

Dear Mr Levinson,

. . . As far as I know, Whitehead never read Wittgenstein. He told me, however, of an encounter with Wittgenstein which was entirely characteristic of the man and may interest you.

The Whiteheads, at my suggestion, invited Wittgenstein for a social tea. Wittgenstein came and, as was his wont, began to silently pace back and forth across the room. Finally, he declared, 'A proposition has two poles; they are apb.' Naturally enough, Whitehead enquired, 'What are a and b?' 'They', replied Wittgenstein with some solemnity, 'are indefinable.'

Yours sincerely
Bertrand Russell

'The Royal Institute of Philosophy is holding a Symposium . . . in honour of the centenary of the birth of Professor A. N. Whitehead. . . . I wonder whether it would be asking you too much to take the Chair on this occasion? . . .'

January 26, 1961

Dear Mr Robertson,
. . . I am very sorry indeed that I cannot be present at the dinner celebrating the centenary of Whitehead's birth as I am already engaged for that time. I should have liked to recall my first meeting with Whitehead in 1877 when his father, as Vicar of the Parish, succeeded in persuading me, more or less, that the earth is round—not to mention subjects of more philosophical importance.

Yours sincerely
Bertrand Russell

'I have read with the greatest interest and enjoyment your *Portraits from Memory.* In it you quote Whitehead as once saying to you: "You think the world is what it looks like in fine weather at noon-day. I think it is what it seems like in the early morning when one first awakes from deep sleep." This statement has so captured my imagination that I have been at last constrained to write to you to ask please could you possibly tell me what exactly he meant by it. . . .'

March 14, 1958

Dear Mr Almond,
Another way of expressing the difference between Whitehead and me is that he thought the world was like a jelly and I thought it was like a heap of shot. In neither case was this a deliberate opinion, but only an imaginative picture. His philosophy in later years was essentially that of Bergson.

Yours sincerely
Bertrand Russell

'The enclosed [paper] will indicate our progress in simulating human problem-solving processes with a computer . . . we obtain rather striking improvements in problem-solving ability . . . in one case [the machine] created a beautifully simple proof to replace a far more complex one in [*Principia*]. . . . The machine required something less than five minutes to find the proof. I am not sure that these facts should be made known to schoolboys. You may also be interested in the evidence of our paper that the learned man and the wise man are not always the same person. . . .'

September 21, 1957

Dear Professor Simon,

Thank you very much for your letter, and for the enclosure. I am delighted by your example of the superiority of your machine to Whitehead and me. I quite appreciate your reasons for thinking that the facts should be concealed from schoolboys. How can one expect them to learn to do sums when they know that machines can do them better? I am also delighted by your exact demonstration of the old saw that wisdom is not the same thing as erudition.

Yours sincerely
Bertrand Russell

'. . . What do *you* consider your greatest contribution to philosophical thought? Your most significant or influential work? What have been your life's objectives? Have you fulfilled them to your satisfaction thus far? . . . What do you predict as the destiny of modern western civilization? What references either by you or about you do you recommend that would lend the greatest insight to the essence of your philosophical thinking? . . .'

March 23, 1962

Dear Mr Duvall,

. . . I find the questions you ask rather difficult to answer. I have attempted in my philosophical work to find that which could be accepted as true and, in so doing, have managed to discover a great deal which had passed for knowledge to be untrue. The tools of analysis which have permitted this I hope have introduced a little clarity. I suppose *Principia Mathematica* might be considered significant. My life's objectives have been broadly to write a series of works which would proceed from abstract to particular truths, and another series from particular to abstract. This I have done. I had hoped to formulate social theory. And this I have done. I had hoped it might be possible to have an influence on public affairs in such manner as to avoid stupidity and malice which characterises so much of human life. In this I have conspicuously failed. I remain convinced that these struggles give meaning and dignity to men's lives and are worthy objectives for them. Modern western civilization seems intent upon elevating its violence to a scale which might be described as global butchery.

My philosophical thinking has changed and varied and I cannot recommend any particular work to you for its essence. Many of the questions you are asking have been answered in books such as *My Philosophical Development*, *Portraits from Memory*, and in an article called 'Reflections on my Eightieth Birthday'.

Yours sincerely
Bertrand Russell

ANEKDOTA

FOREWORD

'My favourite song is Sweet Molly Malone . . .'

The driving curiosity of the public is a particular fate reserved for the famous, and Bertrand Russell was no exception. His photograph and autograph were top priority. His books were purchased and then sent to him for personal signature. Poems were dedicated to him. Sketches and drawings were heaped upon him. Sculptors sent his bust to him. A miscellany of personal data was collected by people of the most divergent interests, hobbies and pursuits—any information able to confirm for an inveterately curious public the fact that a great figure lived and breathed as they do.

Russell obliged with good humour, never falsely elevating his tastes, never making a fetish out of his preferences—although he was rather definite about his brand of whisky. *Sweet Molly Malone* really was his favourite song, and Lord John Russell's pudding his favourite recipe, although he had never tasted it. With a touch of irreverence these join the chosen fads of the famous, painstakingly recorded for posterity by an ever-faithful public. With the Sunday painters Russell was equally tolerant, occasionally allowing himself the indulgence of a minor suggestion: '. . . I have signed the sketch but I very much hope that you will reconsider the shape of the nose.'

Russell was very much in the public domain. He was not merely the property of those organizations connected with the nuclear disarmament movement. Under the slogan 'Greek marbles must go home!' his support was sought by a committee demanding the return of the Elgin Marbles. As with all saints, nothing was spared sanctification. His necktie was requisitioned for display and sale, alongside the ties and cravats of other famous men, at a 'Ties of Friendship' exposition. To all, Russell's response was sympathetic and helpful. The hostile letters, and there are vast quantities of these, were never taken personally. They were answered with great aplomb and pith, and the answers always managed to be constructive.

165

Through letters such as these, interesting sidelights to Russell's personality are uncovered: fragments of information, reminiscences and anecdotes which the public have collectively pried loose. Pieced together they open a rare window on Russell, not the famous man, but the flesh and blood human being. These letters, peppered with witticisms, go far in revealing the depth of Bertrand Russell's personal goodness, warmth and sensitivity.

'. . . I am editing a cookery book consisting of recipes donated by world-famous people. . . . We would be most honoured if you would contribute to this cookery book by letting us have your favourite recipe. . . .'

June 15, 1960

Dear Miss Hellman,

. . . my favourite recipe is for 'Lord John Russell's pudding' which used to occur in *Mrs. Beeton.* I have never tasted the pudding or even seen it, but I choose it from nepotal piety.

Yours sincerely
Bertrand Russell

'. . . I am finding out about words . . . tell me the twenty words that you like most. . . .'

April 7, 1958

Dear Mr Davis,

. . . You ask what are my twenty favourite words. I had never before asked myself such a question, but since your letter came I have made a list which at another time would probably be quite different, so you must not take it very seriously. The list is as follows:

1. Wind
2. Heath
3. Golden
4. Begrime
5. Pilgrim
6. Quagmire
7. Diapason
8. Alabaster
9. Chrysoprase
10. Astrolabe
11. Apocalyptic
12. Ineluctable
13. Terraqueous
14. Inspissated
15. Incarnadine
16. Sublunary
17. Chorasmian
18. Alembic
19. Fulminate
20. Ecstasy

Yours sincerely
Bertrand Russell

'. . . let me know which hymns have stayed most with you since childhood and make some comment on what associations or value they have for you. . . .'

August 5, 1967

Dear Mrs Lunggren,
    . . . When I was a child, we always had family prayers at which a hymn was sung, varying from day to day. As a result, my knowledge of hymns is very considerable. I remember in particular two hymns, of which I quote parts on a separate sheet. Both are from 'Hymns Ancient and Modern'.
    I have always considered these hymns typical of Christian pacifism.

Yours sincerely
Bertrand Russell

Christian, dost thou see them on the holy ground,
How the troops of Midian prowl and prowl around?
Christian, up and smite them, counting gain not loss;
Smite them by the merit of the Holy Cross.

The Son of God goes forth to war,
A Kingly crown to gain;
His blood-red banners stream afar,
Who follows in His train?

(I suppose the answer should be, the Americans in Vietnam.)

'. . . Please accept the little offprint enclosed as a gift from me—it might possibly interest you.'

September 14, 1959

Dear Bredsdorff,
    Thank you for your letter and for your article on 'Nonsense in the Nursery'. Some of the rhymes are variants of the ones that I have always known. Here is a variant of one that you quote on page 340:

Onery twoery tuckerby seven
Allerby crackerby tenaby 'leven
Pin pan musky Dan
Twiddle-um Twaddle-um Twenty-one

On page 348 you have a rhyme made up on a pattern of which I know a different version:

I saw a peacock with a fiery tail
I saw a comet shower down hail,
I saw the heavens begirt with ivy round
I saw a sturdy oak crawling on the ground
I saw a pismire swallow up a whale
I saw the raging seas brim full of ale
I saw a glass full fifty-fathoms deep
I saw a well brim full of tears that men did weep
I saw men's eyes like unto a raging fire
I saw a house as high as the moon and higher
I saw the sun at twelve o'clock at night
I saw the man who saw this wondrous sight

On page 353, the second line about the Old Man of the Abruzzi has always been known to me as so *fat* etc. On page 361 I have always heard the last two lines about Miss Beale and Miss Buss as:

How different from us
Miss Beale and Miss Buss. . . .

Yours sincerely
Bertrand Russell

'. . . I am 14 years old. . . . One of my hobbies is collecting the names of the favorite songs of famous people. . . .'

October 19, 1962

Dear Mark Evans,

Thank you very much for your letter. My favourite song is "Sweet Molly Malone" who sings of the streets of London.

With good wishes,

Yours sincerely
Bertrand Russell

'. . . If it is at all possible, I would appreciate your sending me an autographed picture of you. Also advise if there were a book that particularly influenced your life. Please tell of some that you enjoyed during your childhood days. . . .'

December 8, 1965

Dear Mr Ellisor,

The books I enjoyed most as a child were those of Lewis Carroll and Edward Lear. I do not know of any book that especially influenced me.

I enclose a signed photograph.

Yours sincerely
Bertrand Russell

Russell writes to several booksellers in search of a Latin text book:

September, 1955

Dear Sirs,

I wonder whether you can help me out in the following matter. When I learnt Latin—which was seventy years ago—my text book in grammar was called *Principia Latina*. It contained a number of mnemonic verses such as:

Common are to either sex
Artifex and opifex.
Masculine are fons and mons
Calebs, hydrops, gryps and pons.

There was also the line which political opponents applied to Sir William Harcourt:

Elephas, mas, gigas, as.

There were also the lines

Substantives in -do and -go
Genus fiminimum show;
But ligo, ordo, praedo, cardo
Are masculine; and common, margo.

There were a number of other verses which I can no longer remember. I shall be very grateful if you can find me a Latin grammar containing the above verses. I shall be best pleased if it is *Principia Latina* on which I wasted so much fruitless labour.

Yours sincerely
Bertrand Russell

'We . . . are relieved to learn that the original case of Red Hackle despatched to you . . . has eventually won its way through to you after a delay . . . in transit. . . . In the event of you being over-stocked with Whisky we shall be only too pleased to uplift the second case at our expense. . . .'

July 8, 1960
Dear Sirs,

Thank you for your very pleasant letter of 29 June. You kindly offer to take back part of our supply of Red Hackle if we find our-selves over-stocked. But that is a state of affairs which we cannot believe to be possible. We shall get through the extra supply all too soon.

Yours faithfully
Bertrand Russell

August 2, 1963

Dear Sirs,

My house in London was recently entered by a burglar. He found two bottles of Red Hackle, consumed them on the spot, and thereupon considered further depredations unnecessary. I consider this a tribute to Red Hackle and accordingly I owe you a debt of gratitude.

Will you kindly send me two dozen bottles of Red Hackle to the above address in North Wales.

Yours faithfully
Bertrand Russell

'. . . We are pleased to receive your letter of the 2nd instant requesting a further two dozen bottles of Red Hackle Scotch Whisky. . . . We regret to learn of the "visit" you had from a burglar but it is gratifying to know that his haul only consisted of two bottles of Red Hackle. He must have been truly satisfied with his drink that made further investigation unnecessary.'

'. . . I'd appreciate your general reaction to [*The Restoration of Health*].'

May 19, 1965

Dear Mr Flatto,

Many thanks for sending me your book on *The Restoration of Health.* I am a little behind the times in adopting new maxims of eating or general behaviour as yesterday was my ninety-third birthday. I am quite willing to believe in the correctness of the regimens you recommend, but, as I have smoked a pipe almost continuously for seventy-three years, I do not feel like now surrendering this pleasure.[1] Your pictures of various desirable

[1] Russell has smoked but one brand of tobacco, namely 'Golden Mixture' manufactured by Fribourg and Treyer, of which establishment he has been a customer since 1895.

attitudes are attractive, and I do not doubt all of us would do better if we followed your maxims.

Yours sincerely
Bertrand Russell

'. . . Do you as an atheist celebrate Christmas? . . .'

December 29, 1964

Dear Miss Baker,

Thank you very much for your letter. I attach no religious significance to Christmas, but I find it a pleasant custom and in no way see the need to avoid celebrating it because I grant it no ritualistic importance. . . .

Yours sincerely
Bertrand Russell

'The writer of this letter is a lecturer in English at the Philosophical Faculty at the Budapest University of Sciences. . . . I take the liberty to ask Your Lordship to let me know how you pass the time from getting up in the morning until the evening hours. . . .'

March 26, 1963

Dear Dr Laczer,

. . . From 8 to 11.30 a.m. I deal with my letters and with the newspapers. I receive on an average one hundred letters a day. From 11.30 to 1 p.m. I am seeing people. From 2 to 4 p.m. I read, primarily current nuclear writings. From 4 to 7 p.m. I am writing or seeing people. From 8 to 1 a.m. I am reading and writing. That is my daily routine and I hope it answers your questions.

With good wishes,

Yours sincerely
Bertrand Russell

'I am Housemaster of one of the six houses in this new school . . . we have named our House after you. . . . If you could find time to write to us; could spare any copies of your countless works . . . it would be a great encouragement for this small section of our school population to hear from you. . . .'

November 2, 1966

Dear Mr Ure,

When I first read about Russell House, I had visions of hundreds of boys taking so much interest in my work that they would, in time, be able to come and help me with the hundreds of letters which I receive and must try to answer. Only the absence of such help explains the lateness of this letter.

I enclose a short work which I hope will be of interest, and have asked my secretary to send other items.

With good wishes,

Yours sincerely
Bertrand Russell

———————————

'. . . 1. What are your thoughts during the night when you don't sleep?

2. Have you particular dreams which have to do with professional activities? If so, could you give an example of one which appears to you characteristic?

3. Have dreams furnished you with ideas useful in life? . . .'

October 16, 1958

Dear Sir,

In reply to your letter of October 13, my answers are as follows:

1. When I do not sleep, it is usually because I am kept awake by thinking of foolish things I have done. I try to banish such thoughts by reciting poetry to myself.

2. I never dream about anything concerned with my professional occupation.

3. I have never had a dream which helped me to solve any difficulty in my work, but I have had dreams which cured me of some unconscious piece of self-deception.

> *Yours truly*
> *Bertrand Russell*

'.. Any light that you may be able to shed on [the origin of the soul] would be highly appreciated. We ... enclose a self-addressed envelope and an American postage stamp.'

December 15, 1958

Dear Sirs,

I do not know the origin of belief in the soul, but I suspect it came from dreams. I am returning the stamp which you so kindly sent as American stamps are not yet accepted in England. ...

> *Yours truly*
> *Bertrand Russell*

'I have just bought your *In Praise of Idleness* for someone who is *it* personified! ... He is a man of 58 and is perfectly able to *work* but admits the thought even hurts him! He professes ill health and bores all and sundry about how wonderful he is. Actually his mind is mediocre—his thoughts are others' thoughts, his words are many and meaningless, his deeds are in his imagination only. He is the laziest, stupidest, most greedy, hypocritical being that ever was. ... He spends all his days writing doggerel and sending it all over the world in the hope of preventing war. ... Well, how does one make an idler like that pull up his socks? ...'

December 21, 1961

Dear Madam,

... I hope you will be honest enough to extend to the person whose laziness you describe my complete support and sympathy.

175

Were I nagged day in and day out as he appears to be I should abandon non-violence.

> *Yours faithfully*
> *Bertrand Russell*

'. . . What kind of an Idiot you are can easily be seen by reading some of your so-called philosophy. The other day I read something in a Swiss-German Newspaper you evidently have said:

"We are now living in a period with three revolutions ahead of us: the fight of youth against old age; the fight of poorness against richness and the fight of the fool against intelligency . . ."

. . . The 3 revolutions that are disturbing your mind are definitely not lying ahead of us, but have marked all generations throughout the centuries.

[from] . . . just an ordinary Swiss-fellow, no Lord and no Philosopher'

August 30, 1958

Dear Sir,

There is a kind of idiot that you have not considered. It is the kind which believes what it reads in the newspapers. I never made any such statement as you quote.

> *Yours truly*
> *Bertrand Russell*

'. . . Mr Russell, what do you think of marriage between older, mellow, and brilliant men such as yourself, and young, cheerful girls with fairly sound teeth—like me? . . .'

November 28, 1964

Dear Miss Murray,

Thank you very much for your kind letter. I am already married—happily. . . .

With good wishes,

Yours sincerely
Bertrand Russell

'I wish to offer you my Congratulations on your courageous stand over the H. Bomb. . . . As an O[ld] A[ge] P[ensioner] I do a little sketching as a hobby, and would esteem it a great honour if you would autograph the enclosed sketch. . . .'

October 2, 1961

Dear Mr Spence,

I have signed the sketch, but I very much hope that you will reconsider the shape of the nose.

Yours sincerely
Bertrand Russell

'. . . We intend to feature a "Ties of Friendship" display which will be world-wide in appeal. We aim to acquire one tie, or if you wish cravat, from the leading personalities in the world, with a short letter accompanying each. These ties will then be . . . sold to the highest bidder. The monies obtained therefrom will be used in furthering the objectives of our Order which are "Peace, Brotherly Love and Harmony". . . .'

March 15, 1960

To: The 10th Annual Spring Bazaar and Carnival
B'nai B'rith,
Automotive Building, Exhibition Park,
Toronto.

I send you with this tie that I have worn my best wishes for the success of your Annual Exposition and for the furtherance of the objectives of your Order—'Peace, Brotherly Love and Harmony' –with which I am in very warm sympathy.

Yours faithfully
Bertrand Russell

A FERVENT APPEAL
'JUSTICE IS THE SUM TOTAL OF ALL VIRTUES'—PLUTARCH

At a time when Justice and good will are subjects close to the hearts of all of us, and freedom within law and order looms before us as an indispensable force, we appeal to the people of the English Commonwealth, and especially to the intellectuals of England, to do justice to the Mother of Art, to Eternal Hellas, to do all they can in their power for the return of the stolen works of art, taken away from the place of their birth. Our cause is based on justice and fair play, and will eventually prove successful because universal public opinion is on our side.

Gratefully,

THE COMMITTEE FOR THE RETURN OF THE ELGIN MARBLES TO GREECE

'Greece needs your assistance. The greatest wrong must be righted. Greek marbles must go home.'

February 15, 1963

Dear Mr Xynidis,

Thank you for your letter. I agree that the Elgin Marbles should be returned, although I do not feel, as you do, that it is the 'greatest wrong'.

With good wishes,

Yours sincerely
Bertrand Russell

'. . . I understand that you are about to publish a book on the Eichmann case. Permit me to send you the enclosed paper I wrote. . . .'

December 28, 1961

Dear Professor Zeisel,

Thank you for your letter and for the enclosed paper. I found it of genuine interest, but I am afraid that you have confused me with Lord Russell of Liverpool. Recently the two of us wrote a letter to the London *Times* pointing out that each of us was not the other.

I wish you success with your paper.

Yours sincerely
Bertrand Russell

'. . . I have a black and white print entitled "The Trial of William Lord Russell at the Old Bailey". . . . Could you please tell me if he is a relative of the present Lord Russell?'

September 28, 1963

Dear Mr Groom,
. . . William Lord Russell was, indeed, my ancestor. He provided me with an example, only I was not deprived of my head as a result of my own day at the Old Bailey. . . .

Yours sincerely
Bertrand Russell

'Dear Sir Bertrand,
  You will enjoy reading Robert Perkin's column . . . also find enclosed . . . my picture . . . my face is quite different from that of the lad you . . . encouraged at Harvard many years ago. . . .'

February 11, 1958

Dear Mr Aandahl,
Thank you for your letter of February 2 and for the nice photograph of yourself and also for the very pleasing cutting from the *Rocky Mountain News*. If you see Mr. Perkin I should be glad if you would convey my thanks to him. By the way, I am not 'Sir Bertrand'. 'Sir' is a title confined to Baronets and Knights, neither of which I am. Nor am I 'Lord Bertrand'. For public purposes, I am 'Bertrand Russell'; and privately I am 'Lord Russell'. In addressing a letter or in a formal document, I am 'Earl Russell' —but the word 'Earl' is not used in conversation. I am sure all these complications must appear to you as ridiculous as they are, and for my part I do not care a pin how I am addressed. . . .

Yours sincerely
Bertrand Russell

'. . . It would be of immense help to me if you would kindly let me have your views . . . about the present function of the House [of Lords] and its work in the future. . . .'

September 7, 1963

Dear Mr Franklin,

Thank you very much for your letter. I consider the House of Lords to be otiose and entirely without serious effect. I favour its abolition.

With good wishes,

Yours sincerely
Bertrand Russell

'. . . It has been one of my dreams for a long, long time to erect a statue of Thomas Paine in London to memorialize Paine's writing of *The Rights of Man*. If you think that there is a probability of using your influence to get the City of London to give us a site, I would gladly assume the responsibility of raising the money for the statue. . . .'

August 10, 1960

Dear Mr Lewis,

I am sorry that I have no influence with the officials of the City of London, and if I approached them to advocate your project, I should ensure its rejection. I am afraid therefore that I can do nothing for you. The government of the City consists of rich men who, for the most part, are pious, considering that they have reason to thank God for their blessings.

Yours sincerely
Bertrand Russell

'. . . Could you possibly let me know if your educational experiment has been reported upon by anybody. . . .'

January 24, 1959

Dear Mr Francis,

. . . I do not know of any literature about the school that I ran for a while and I do not think there is anything interesting to be said about it. The running of a school, as I quickly discovered, requires practical and administrative talents which I do not possess.

Yours truly
Bertrand Russell

'In Webster's *Dictionary of Synonyms* I find the following quotation, attributed to you, used to illustrate the correct use of both "intrinsic" and "intellectual": "The knowledge of geographical facts is useful, but without intrinsic intellectual value."

'. . . There are still many people who deny that geography has any intrinsic intellectual value, and who regard geographers as so many academic charlatans. Must we number you among our detractors? . . .'

February 28, 1959

Dear Mr Duncan,
 . . . I do not know where I made the statement about geographical facts which you quote. Indeed, I do not remember to have made it. Clearly the emphasis is on the word 'facts'. When I was taught geography as a child, I was made to learn the names of the Capes on the coast of England in their order and I had to get by heart a list of the principal towns with their exports and imports. I discovered that as regards exports it was safe to say 'hardware', though I had not the least idea what the word meant. After I ceased to be taught geography I began to find it very interesting, but it is rather the interconnection of facts than the isolated facts that seems to me of value. I still think that it is just to say of the isolated facts of geography that they have little *intrinsic* intellectual value (I think few facts have), but I most emphatically do not regard geographers as academic charlatans. When I was still young, I was led to the opposite view by H. J. McKinder.

Yours sincerely
Bertrand Russell

'... In a General Knowledge Quiz set by my school I have to find the answer to the following question:
What remarkable physical feat was performed by Earl Russell? I have been unable to find any reference anywhere. ...'

January 2, 1960

Dear Miss Yarnton,
The remarkable physical feat which I suppose to be in question was mainly a journalistic invention. I was a passenger in a plane which sank in the fjord at Trondheim. Some of the passengers were killed. The rest had to jump out and swim about a hundred yards to a nearby boat. The newspapers exaggerated everything.[1]
Yours truly
Bertrand Russell

'... I am especially embarrassed by the manner in which America treated you. That is one of the most shameful pages in American history. ... I don't know if I have it in me or not, but someday before I die I'm going to write a book entitled, *The Influence of Bertrand Russell on America.* ... You will leave the world a much better place than you found it. At least with the hopes of becoming a much better place. The enclosed page from yesterday's *Denver Post* indicates that even America is beginning to recognize your wisdom and statesmanship—at long last. ...'

August 22, 1958

Dear Mr Aandahl,
Thank you for your most agreeable letter of August 14 which it was a great pleasure to get. Thank you also for the cutting from the *Denver Post.* I was only once in Denver, and that was in the days of Judge Ben B. Lindsey whom your city did not treat very kindly. I gather from you that it has since become more liberal.
I look forward to your promised book about my influence on

[1] Although the newspapers exaggerated, Russell's description is too modest; the event alluded to took place in 1948 when he was 76.

America. My first lectures in your country were in 1896, and my last in 1951, so I have had a fairly long experience of the United States.

I wish I could believe that I shall leave the world a better place than I found it. So far, the opposite seems more probable. I thank you once again for your letter which is a real encouragement to me.

Yours sincerely
Bertrand Russell

'I am engaged . . . on a large-scale musical-biographical study of the late Ralph Vaughan Williams. Knowing that you were contemporary with him at Cambridge, I wonder if you have any memory of him in those days which you might care to tell me about? . . .'

November 25, 1961

Dear Mr Kennedy,

. . . I knew Ralph Vaughan Williams well when he was an undergraduate, though not as well as I knew his cousin Ralph Wedgwood. I was very fond of Ralph Vaughan Williams who was in those days a most determined atheist and was noted for having walked into Hall one evening saying in a loud voice, 'Who believes in God now-a-days, I should like to know?' I hardly ever saw him in later years, though I retained an affectionate admiration for him. I am sorry that I have not more to tell you.

Yours sincerely
Bertrand Russell

'I am writing a book on Edward Carpenter, the nineteenth century mystic poet and social reformer. . . . I gather Carpenter was an admirer of your work during the first world war. I am interested in knowing your attitude to his work in general, and his books on sex and mysticism in particular. . . .'

184

October 29, 1964

Dear Mr Barua,

. . . My connection with Edward Carpenter was very slight. When I was twenty-one, I was a good deal influenced by some booklets that he wrote concerning sex, but I never liked his mysticism. The only time that I met him was at a conference on votes for women at Edinburgh. Some of us were invited to stay with Bartholomew, the inventor of Bartholomew's $\frac{1}{2}$ inch maps. Among those staying with him were Edward Carpenter and Mrs. Fawcett, the leader of the constitutional branch of women's suffrage. Mrs. Fawcett refused to speak to Edward Carpenter, because he advocated a humane attitude to homosexuality, which caused inconvenience to everybody else. I have never read any of his poetry, nor, indeed, any of his writing except the booklets that I mentioned, but on the one occasion that I met him, at Bartholomew's, I liked him.

Yours sincerely
Bertrand Russell

'. . . My purpose in writing to you is to ask you one or two questions about the late T. S. Eliot. I am aware that he was a student of yours years ago at Harvard, and that you introduced him to a number of people in London, later. . . . Could you possibly give me any anecdotes or information about him? His friends all seem to think that he was the epitome of goodness and morality, but his writings seem to me to display an astonishing narrowmindedness and intolerance. . . .'

March 9, 1965

Dear Mr Gonin,

I entirely agree with your estimate of Eliot's character. I made his acquaintance in the Spring of 1914 while teaching a graduate class of which he was a member. I happened to say that I admired Heraclitus, to which he replied in a dreamy tone, 'Yes, he's so like Villon.' This was the only remark he made to me during those three months, but it caused me to remember him when I met him by chance just after the beginning of the First War in London in October. I said, 'Hello, what are you doing here?' He said, 'I have just returned from Berlin.' I said, 'What do you think of the war?' He said, 'I don't know, except that I'm not a pacifist.' I said, 'I see. You don't care what people are killed about, so long as they are killed.'

Yours truly
Bertrand Russell

'. . . it occurred to me that you might possibly have some personal knowledge of a man whose life and work I have been studying for some years—George Gissing, the Victorian novelist who died in 1903. I wonder if you remember any of his books being first published and, if you never met him yourself, if you knew any-one—perhaps H. G. Wells—who knew him personally and ever mentioned him to you? . . .'

February 11, 1958

Dear Mr Mansley,
    I never met Gissing though I read most of his novels with con-siderable admiration. I think the only fact I can contribute that might be of interest to you is one that I learnt from H. G. Wells. In Wells's novel *Tono Bungay* a somewhat rascally financier dies a very edifying death which seems out of character. I asked Wells about this and he told me that he had utilized his notes on Gissing's last illness and death—a somewhat odd proceeding.

Yours sincerely
Bertrand Russell

'I am writing to you in the hope that you will consent to help me with my work on the late Sinclair Lewis. . . . Your recollections of the man and his work would be invaluable. Any bit of informa-tion or anecdote you could contribute to illuminate his persona-lity, his opinions and attitudes would be deeply appreciated. . . .'

September 7, 1957

Dear Mr Friedman,

I am sorry I cannot tell you as much as you evidently hope. . . . I remember two things about Sinclair Lewis. First: after an hour's monologue, during which he had refused one the chance to saying a word, he could tell, with perfect and exact mimicry, precisely what one would have said if he had given one a chance. Second: we played a game in which one person was sent out of the room, the others agreed on a poet, and on the person's return into the room he was told that he must answer all questions in the style of that poet. We sent Sinclair Lewis out of the room and decided on Swinburne. He answered all questions in perfect Swinburnian style. My remaining recollections of him are not fit to print. . . .

Yours sincerely
Bertrand Russell

'. . . At the moment we are studying the works of D. H. Lawrence and the other day I read that you were once friendly with him. Please would you tell me something about him? What did he believe in? What kind of man was he? . . .'

October 22, 1962

Dear Miss Roberts,

. . . Lawrence was a man who was consumed with a desire to punish [those] who did not share his intense feelings, borne of personal conflict and a wish to do violence he hated rationality and emphasised violent feeling—'thinking with the blood'.

He was a remarkable man but not a likable one. He believed in the dominance of strong emotion about which he was not very clear and he felt industrial life and social convention stifled natural urges. He also felt this was true of intellectual rigour. His difficulty in coming to terms with the extremity of his feelings made him despise ordinary men and women because they did not seem to experience the same. Such impulses may create striking imaginative work but not a man who can see the world as possibly having merit apart from his own private experience.

187

You will find that I have recorded some personal experience of D. H. Lawrence in my book *Portraits From Memory*.

Yours sincerely
Bertrand Russell

'. . . I am writing a programme about D. H. Lawrence. . . . The main interest of the programme is to lie in this question: was Lawrence persecuted, or did he go out of his way to annoy the authorities? . . .'

September 11, 1957

Dear Mr Butler,

I am sorry that I have not anything of value to contribute to your discussion as to whether Lawrence was persecuted. I do not think he was provocative, but I think his wife was. I was informed on good authority (though I cannot vouch for the story) that when Zeppelins came over she used to go onto Hampstead Heath and cheer. Lawrence himself, I think, tried to avoid annoying the authorities, but I do not know enough to say anything publicly.

Yours truly
Bertrand Russell

'. . . I am greatly interested to learn that Tagore visited you three times, and I should very much like to know what you personally felt about him on these occasions. . . . I see that Lowes Dickinson speaks of one of these meetings in the 22/2/1923 issue of *New Leader*:

' "It is a June evening, in a Cambridge garden. Mr. Bertrand Russell and myself sit there alone with Tagore. He sings to us some of his poems, the beautiful voice and the strange mode floating away on the gathering darkness. Then Russell begins to talk, coruscating like lightning in the dusk. Tagore falls into silence. But afterwards he said, it had been wonderful to hear Russell talk. He had passed into a 'higher state of consciousness' and heard it, as it were, from a distance. What, I wonder, had he heard?"

'What indeed did Tagore hear on that evening? According to another article (*The Nation*, 18/7/25), he uttered the following words next morning:

' "The truth is that in that hallowed enclosure, I quickly passed into the second state of consciousness, and experienced absorbing apprehensions. I do not remember a word of what the Professor said, though my ear listened intently, and appreciated the facility of his method. But it was all entirely irrelevant to the important matters of life and devoid of scientific discernment of demonstrably accessible facts."

'I wonder if you remember anything about this particular meeting? . . .'

February 16, 1963

Dear Mr Chatterji,

 . . . I recall the meeting of which Lowes Dickinson writes only vaguely. There was an earlier occasion, the first upon which I met Tagore, when he was brought to my home by Robert Trevelyan and Lowes Dickinson. I confess that his mystic air did not attract me and I recall wishing he would be more direct. He had a soft, rather elusive, manner which led one to feel that straightforward exchange or communication was something from which he would shy away. His intensity was impaired by his self-absorption. Naturally, his mystic views were by way of dicta and it was not possible to reason about them.

With good wishes,

Yours sincerely
Bertrand Russell

'For nearly three years now I have been at work on William Faulkner's official biography. I have done research in Stockholm on the Nobel Prize ceremonies of 1950. I am trying now to obtain information from others who were there then. . . .'

September 29, 1965

Dear Professor Blotner,

. . . The only time when I have met Faulkner was at the Nobel Prize ceremonies of 1950. I thought he felt himself out of place in the atmosphere of Royalty, trumpets and general grandeur. I therefore tried to make friends with him, but found it uphill work as he was shy and reticent. Like the rest of us, he had to make a speech, but it was totally inaudible. The only impression that I carried away was that it is difficult for kings to be kind to rebels.

Yours sincerely
Bertrand Russell

'. . . Particularly valuable for my work are your reactions to Conrad. . . . In *Portraits from Memory* you describe your remarkable rapport. . . .'

October 3, 1961

Dear Mr Watts,

. . . As for the strange sympathy between Conrad and myself, I cannot pretend that I have ever quite understood it. I think I have always felt that there were two levels, one that of science and common sense, and another, terrifying, subterranean and periodic, which in some sense held more truth than the everyday view. You might describe this as a Satanic mysticism. I have never been convinced of its truth, but in moments of intense emotion it overwhelms me. It is capable of being defended on the most pure intellectual grounds—for example, by Eddington's contention that the laws of physics only *seem* to be true because of the things that we choose to notice. I suppose that the feeling I had for Conrad depended upon his combination of passion and pessimism—but that perhaps is a simplification. You ask whether my feeling for Conrad was based upon a common sense of loneliness. I think this may have been the case, but the experience, while it lasted, was too intense for analysis.

Yours sincerely
Bertrand Russell

'. . . I thought you would be interested in my discoveries concerning Shelley. . . .'

July 25, 1960

Dear Mr Dowling,

Thank you very much for sending me your very interesting investigation of the attack on Shelley at Tanyrallt. Ever since, as an adolescent, I became interested in Shelley, this story has intrigued me, and now that I live in full view of Tanyrallt[1] my interest has received a fresh stimulus. I am quite persuaded by your reconstruction and I congratulate you on unearthing the man Leeson. I did not know that already then there was a peer

'. . . who brews
a lordlier liquor than the Muse.'

I think perhaps, even now, the neighbouring gentry might have some difficulty in welcoming an ardent young Communist who had been sent down from Oxford for atheism and excluded from decent society for preaching free love. But in our degenerate days the gentry are not what they were and the doctrine that virtue is proportional to income has become unfashionable.

I hope that you will get your essay published and, if you do, I shall be very grateful for a copy of it.

Yours sincerely
Bertrand Russell

P.S. (Remembering what Shelley said about Castlereagh)

I met a furious cruel villain
He looked to me just like MacMillan.

I think that perhaps even now this sentiment might not be welcomed by the gentry of North Wales.

---

[1] Across the estuary from Russell's home, Plas Penrhyn, Penrhyndeudraeth in Wales.

TAILPIECE

May, 1968

Dear Mr Feinberg and Mr Kasrils,

Thank you very much for sending me your collection of my letters from 1950 to 1968. I have seldom come across a book that delighted me more and I earnestly hope that it will be published. . . . I read it at once on receipt of it.

Some of the letters especially delight me, notably the one from Paul Altmann, a six year old. I was also much pleased by a letter on education which expresses my views more succinctly than they are generally expressed. The belief which I state in that letter is the opposite of that held by most educators: namely, education should encourage the young to question what has been taken for granted.

It seems to me that your choice of letters is admirable and gives a very just picture of my opinions at various dates. I also think your editing and notes and the forewords to each section are excellent. And I like the title! . . .

Yours sincerely
Bertrand Russell

INDEX

Malinovsky, Marshall, 68
Manchester Guardian, 105
'Man's Peril', 26, 66–7
Marriage and Morals, 23, 109, 124, 146, 150, 152–3
Marx, 141, 145
marxism, 88–9, 140
McCarthyism, 26
McKinder, Sir H. J., 182
McNamara, Robert, 69
Methuselah, 119
militarism, 92–3
Mill, John Stuart, 21
Mind, 156
Mohammed, 57
Morrell, Lady Ottoline, 22
Moscow, 65
Munich, 24
Murray, Gilbert, 22
Mussolini, 82
'My Own Philosophy', 124
My Philosophical Development, 28, 135, 158, 162
'My Religious Reminiscences', 39–40

Nation, The, 189
national socialism, 24
NATO, 68–9, 98, 126
nazis, 54, 92, 144
Nehru, Jawaharlal, 18, 28, 63, 82
Neill, A. S., 108
New Hopes for a Changing World, 128
New Leader, 188
Nightmares of Eminent Persons, 28
Nobel Prize, 17, 25, 189–90

Old Bailey, 179–80
Order of Merit, 25
Our Knowledge of the External World, 137, 154

pacifism, 91, 143
Paine, Thomas, 181

Palestine, 83
Pascal, 157
Passionate Sceptic, The, 113
patriotism, 116
Peano, Guiseppe, 156
Pearsall Smith, Alys (*see* Alys Russell)
Peking University, 23
Pentagon, 72, 75, 94
Plas Penrhyn, Penrhyndeudraeth, 191
Poincaré, Henri, 156
Political Ideals, 142
Portraits from Memory, 65–6, 92, 104, 145, 162, 188, 190
Power, A New Social Analysis, 140
Practice and Theory of Bolshevism, The, 23, 145
Principia Mathematica, 21, 56, 123–5, 135, 158, 161
Principles of Social Reconstruction, 124
Problem of China, The, 109
Problems of Philosophy, 139
Pugwash, 26–7, 66

Rabinovitch, Eugene, 67
Rákosi, Mátyás, 26
'Red Hackle', 171–2
'Reflections on my 80th Birthday', 162
Republic, The, 130
Rights of Man, The, 181
Rochester, Bishop of, 56
Rocky Mountain News, 180
Rosenberg, Julius & Ethel, 26
Rousseau, Jean Jaques, 157
Rusk, Dean, 69
Russell, Alys (née Pearsall Smith), 21
Russell, Conrad, 24
Russell, Dora (née Black), 23
Russell, Edith (née Finch), 19, 25
Russell, Frank, 21
Russell, John Conrad, 23